Catholic
Means
Universal

D0062563

Catholic
Means
Universal

INTEGRATING SPIRITUALITY AND RELIGION

David Richo, Ph.D.

A Crossroad Book
The Crossroad Publishing Company
New York

The Crossroad Publishing Company
370 Lexington Avenue, New York, NY 10017

Printed in the United States of America

Library of Congress Cataloging-in-Publication Data

Richo, David, 1940-
    Catholic means universal : integrating spirituality and religion /
by David Richo.
        p.   cm.
    Includes bibliographical references.
    ISBN 0-8245-1837-3 (pbk.)
    1. Spirituality.   2. Spiritual life – Catholic Church.
3. Psychology, Religious.   4. Nature – Religious aspects.
5. Spiritual life (Buddhism)   I. Title.
BL624.R55 2000
291.4 – dc21   99–39020

1   2   3   4   5   6   7   8   9   10   06   05   04   03   02   01   00

To Mary of Mount Carmel:
Mother of all the living,
Cause of joy,
Who asked me to love as she does,
and to my sister Lois,
who keeps showing me how.
I cherish both of you with love and thanks.

I am a pilgrim of the future on my way back from a journey
made entirely in the past....
May the Lord only preserve in me
a passionate taste for the world.

— PIERRE TEILHARD DE CHARDIN

Modern man... has lost the protection of ecclesiastical walls
erected and reinforced so carefully since Roman days,
and because of this loss
has approached the zone of world-creating fire.

— CARL JUNG

What can I accomplish?
Although not yet a Buddha,
Let my priest's body
Be the raft to carry
Sentient beings to the yonder shore.

— DOGEN ZENJI

Contents

Prologue

Our best chance of finding God is to look in the place where we left him.
— MEISTER ECKHART

I stopped asking why one day and said yes. That opened a door long ago closed, or rather left ajar: my faith. This is not an autobiography, but my story certainly figures in the pages that follow without my telling it directly. I am a formerly active Catholic priest, now a Jungian psychotherapist and teacher on a Buddhist path. I left nothing behind; all has been annexed and integrated. What follows reflects the results of that glad and, at times, painful enterprise. Though this continues as the task of a lifetime, the new millennium seems the time to say: "Well, here goes, world, take a look at what I have found so far."

I present a threefold subject: recovering from the repression of our religious past, retaining the riches of our religion, and redesigning our religion so that our faith can accommodate the advances of our contemporary world. Such an ambitious subject can provide a turning point in appreciating Catholicism and religion in general. To reach so sublime a goal takes some fancy footwork. I propose doing that by partnering theology with a Jungian perspective, Buddhist insights, and the universal wisdom that is reflected again and again in Catholic teachings. The past, so poor, so rich, can be appreciated; the present, so ancient, so new, can be enjoyed. This is how I see the Everything as always and everywhere within reach.

My hope is that this book will be useful to disaffected Catholics who have left the Church and want to see if there is anything of value in religion that can now be integrated into their worldview. It may also be a resource to intelligent Catholics and other Christians who want to upgrade their faith in the light of myth, psychology, and religious traditions. It may also be useful to therapists, spiritual directors, and partners who work or live with Catholics or other Christians. The year 2000 is a jubilee year for Catholicism. Reclaiming our past to enrich our future can make this our personal jubilee year too.

The word "catholic" means universal and inclusive. It is the everything within reach. The universality has many implications. The Church is meant to be catholic in the sense that it honors and draws from all traditions. The Church is catholic in that it presents a universal equation between the natural, the human, and the divine. The Church is catholic when it accommodates, welcomes, and encourages the advances of science and current consciousness. This means that it needs to be continually updating itself in the four main realms of religion: its beliefs are not tied to outmoded dogmatic formulations; its morality is not rigid but prohuman; its rituals are intelligible and relevant to contemporary people; its devotions are theologically based and not superstitious or magical. We do not leave what includes us. Ironically, the reason people cease being Catholic may be because the Church has ceased to be catholic. Spirituality splits from religion when religion ceases to be relevant and updated in the four ways listed above. The chapters that follow attempt to reinstate religion within spirituality by suggesting some possible paths toward catholicity. There are too many riches in our Catholic tradition to let it fade from our lives. We can make a commitment to a catholic renewal of ourselves and our desacralized world. Then our past and our present meet, and that is the meaning of jubilee.

Faith does not have to mean superstition. It does not have to be a substitute for experience but can be a supplement to it. Faith can be an adult enthusiasm that is intimately connected to the works of mercy in the world. It is possible to be simultaneously a Catholic and a humanist in the fullest sense. This "new age" has feared, distrusted, and discarded religion in so many ways. Yet religion can be a friendly force to be included within spirituality and not an antagonist to it. We have heard often: "Spirituality is not religion." We can change that to: "Spirituality is enriched by religion."

We lose so much when we exclude a reality that is innately in us and has inhabited human consciousness since earliest times. To see religion as an institutionalizing of spirituality is a limited perspective. Spirituality has always included the elements of religion: belief, morality, ritual, and devotion. It is time to reinstate these gifts in our spiritual lives.

Religion is usually rejected because of its dualism. I am suggesting that the dualism is a distortion that can be corrected when we perceive a triune ratio: the human inheres in the divine as the divine inheres in the natural. All three are one. A theologian is a depth psychologist is a naturalist and vice versa. This idea has an ancient lineage going back to mystics like Meister Eckhart and linking to modern contributors like Teilhard de Chardin, Thomas Merton, and David Steindl-Rast. St. Francis expressed it in his primordial poem "Brother Sun, Sister...." We are not innovators. We are inheritors, not of a new story but of a whole story..

Catholic Means Universal is meant to be heterodox and challenging, more like the ninety-five theses than an encyclical. I do not intend to be iconoclastic but to respect icons as accurate and comforting mirrors of the depth of our human and natural selves. I intend always to be respectful of where individual readers find themselves on their spiritual journeys.

When St. Peter's life was in danger, he left Rome along the Appian Way. He met a stranger who gradually became recognizable as Jesus, the friend he betrayed and from whom he had found forgiveness. Peter asked him, "Quo vadis, Domine?" "Where are you going, Lord?" The answer he received showed him where he himself needed to go: "If you leave my people behind, I must go back to Rome to die for them again." When Peter heard these words, he began to weep in clear recognition of his true path.

In what follows I attempt to tease out some of the marvels and challenges along the Appian Way of faith. I may present more questions than conclusions. In fact, I see questions as *guides*. Peter's journey to rebirth found direction, after all, in a question from the heart of Jesus to his: "Where are you going?"

> I'm ceded, I've stopped being theirs.
> The name they dropped upon my face
> With water, in the country church
> Is finished using now,
> And They can put it with my dolls,
> My childhood, and the string of spools,
> I've finished threading too.
>
> Baptized, before, without the choice,
> But this time, consciously, of grace —
> Unto supremest name —
> Called to my full — the crescent dropped —
> Existence's whole arc, filled up
> With one small diadem.

My second rank — too small the first —
Crowned — crowing — on my father's breast —
A half-unconscious queen —
But this time, adequate, erect,
With will to choose or to reject,
And I choose: just a Crown —

— Emily Dickinson

ONE

The Paradigms of Our Religious Past

Recovering and Appreciating

Paradoxically, in order to grow beyond an old myth, it is often necessary to accept the role it played in your life, and understand the reasons you at one time embraced it.
— DAVID FEINSTEIN AND STANLEY KRIPPNER,
Personal Mythology: The Psychology of Your Evolving Self

Adult faith is fidelity to our own intuitive experience and to the values and gifts of our religious past. The joyous task of discovery of the riches of our faith also has a painful side requiring a recovery program. Some of our experiences in our childhood religion were positive, life-affirming, and nurturant. Some were hurtful or abusive. The hurts, abuses, and losses of our religious past can turn to bitterness as we dwell on them later. Bitterness is a sign that the healthy anger in grief is still unreleased. Hurts and abuses remain as permanent scars until they are mourned and let go of. Simply leaving the Church or "forgetting" our religious past does not heal us or give us a sense of closure. Healing means integration, and this begins not by forgetting but by remembering what happened to us. Integration happens not by refusing to feel but by feeling more than ever. Integration happens not by antagonism but by reconciliation of our own inner warring oppositions: abiding bonds and broken bonds. Integration happens not by holding on to bitter resentment but by letting go of it and getting on with life.

All these together — remembering, confronting, expressing feelings, and letting go — are part of mourning and healing. We know we need to mourn when we still feel bitterness, resentment, anger, disappointment, or any such strong reaction to our religious past. Mourning is the best way to clear ourselves of all the flotsam of the unfinished past; it is the natural process for resolving the pain and losses of life. It takes time and the timing has to be right, that is, respectful of our personal readiness.

15

Mourning the past and its hurts is a form of self-parenting. Only those who self-parent can form relationships uncontaminated by child-to-parent expectations. Self-parenting is what adults do. As long as we are using the Church to parent us in the way children are parented, we are giving away our power. To grow up religiously is to be self-parenting *and* responsive to the nurturance, guidance, and support of others. Then the Church can be the kind and wise adult parent of an adult, as we see in healthy relationships between adults and their parents. This is how we recover our spiritual dignity.

Renewal of faith in an adult way requires the psychological ingredient of mourning the pain of the past and letting go of it. This brings recovery and moving on. A space opens for us where before there was none. We find the reserves of our own energy and the graces always accessible to us but never fully evoked. We then feel no need to blame or please. Our trust is in our own power to see, name, and handle or avoid abuse.

To grieve as part of our recovery process is to reclaim transcendent support, the graces that we keep noticing or missing everywhere on our journey. This is the spiritual dimension of the work: access to a higher power than our wounded ego. If there was no visible means of supportive love and respectful guidance in childhood, it will be difficult to believe in a God who offers invisible support. This is how early neglect or abuse vitiates and plunders our spirituality. When what hurt us also comforted us, the clarity required for healthy grief is difficult to achieve.

Some of us remember painful moments in our Catholic past. Truly abusive events of the past may still be abusing us — often quite subtly — in the present. We identify abuses by looking for present distress and riding it back to whatever original distress resembles it. For example, we feel particularly wounded when someone ridicules us for our opinion. Our reaction seems out of proportion to the event. That may be a clue that it is reminiscent of an earlier experience of ridicule by a priest or nun for our response in catechism classes. Such abuses can be worked on by mourning: acknowledging our pain, fully feeling our sadness and anger, and letting go when we are able to naturally in our own time.

Remembering abuses means noticing which old injunctions may still be disturbing. It is perfectly normal to be assailed from time to time with guilt, shame, and fears that were conditioned into us in childhood. Everyone has automatic trains of thought that link immediate experience with an old belief, for example, "I'll go to hell if I do this." Such fleeting thoughts may never disappear altogether. They do not harm us unless we become obsessive about them or give up our serenity to suit them. Healthy persons recognize such relics as part of their mental territory, given the misinformation, superstition, and fears originally drilled into our minds when we had no defense against them. School, parents, the media, and many other sources of influence affected us in the same way.

Adults notice the conditioned reflexes of their minds with humor, not bitterness. The inner archaic voice can be quieted over the years, though perhaps never wholly muted. The voice is quieted by repeatedly choosing what we want over and above the inner injunction. This freedom renders the voice harmless so whether it ever becomes mute is irrelevant. (At the same time as adults we discern when guilt, stripped of its linkage to hell, bespeaks an appropriate truth: some appropriate twinge or nudge of conscience that calls for our attention, an action, or an amendment.)

Part of the anger in grief is resentment of anyone who induced guilt in us. Our anger at the Church may be in the fact that we still feel guilty about innocent pleasure, or so it seems. It could be that some of our guilt is not about pleasure, but about *power.* We have dared to defy the authority who proscribed this behavior and whom we believe we are supposed to resent. We have stepped out of line, taken power into our own hands. To do this is scary because it entails risking the loss of approval or endangering the means of survival. Actually, we have explored or exposed a part of ourselves that reveals us to ourselves. We have come to the frontier of a new identity: one that allows us to say no to an external voice in favor of an inner intuitive voice. Identity for adults begins precisely at the point where blind obedience to external imperatives comes to an end and new steps beyond the safe horizons begin. A common theme in myths is that of the hero or heroine who enters the secret room, opens the locked box, or eats the forbidden fruit of knowledge. This knowledge is power, and reclaiming it may be what scares us most of all. The hero is the personification of our urgent desire to individuate no matter what it may take.

It is important to respect our own timing in the process of remembering abuses. We let in only what we can handle as we can handle it. Temporary denial of some of the facts is useful in griefwork because our psyche knows how much we can deal with at one time and lets the information in, little by little, as we become able to stand it. When we are ready to know, we will know. We may never know it all. Only then can we allow a full venting of feelings like sadness, anger, and fear.

In the first stages, remembering and feeling, we do not let the Church off the hook: "They didn't know any better back then." "It's different now." True compassion and forgiveness *follow* the anger and remembrance. The impact of what happened matters most at this point, not the intention of the abusers. We need to experience as much of the impact as we can handle. The understanding of intentions will come later as an automatic result of our griefwork.

We may have felt safe and comfortable in Sister Ursula's first communion class. We still remember what a sweet person she was. But when she implanted dire fears in our seven-year-old minds, she was abusing us. Her intention was not to harm us. But the impact may have been harmful. In griefwork we attend to the impact, not the intention. (And some Sister Ursulas were sweet and not abusive at all!)

Reminiscence means baring the abuse instead of bearing it. It is an admission to ourselves of what happened and what we felt about it. It does not matter if we are accurate in our recollection. We are working on subjective impact, not on historical precision. If we cannot remember specific events, we can perhaps remember our sense of it all. Even that is sufficient at this first stage. We avoid asking, "Why did this happen?" We have always been consoled by explanations and such consolation can be a distraction. We go directly to the fact as a given. We change the why to a yes. *The past has to be so thoroughly excavated that the frozen energies buried in it can be retrieved and reinvested in the present.*

Part of the abuse cycle is learning to dissociate. Dissociation can be described in this way: while we are being abused, physically, sexually, or emotionally, we become numb to the hurt and pain that is happening to us. Unconsciously and automatically, we "turn off" the stimulus and take flight into fantasy or distracting behavior. This dissociation has a wisdom in it because it helps us bear the pain without being overwhelmed by it. Such dissociation accounts for the fact that later in life we forget the abuses that happened to us. Part of the work of mourning is reassociating with the occluded vision of our pain. What was necessary and wise in the past is no longer so in the present. We now allow ourselves to know our hurts and others' abuses of us in order to clear our path to healing.

The result of knowing and grieving will be to shift our focus from how we were victimized to a disidentification with the victim role. The healthy version of dissociation (denial) is disidentification (freedom from the sense of oneself as a victim). This may not happen at this early stage, but it will happen in the course of griefwork (recalling, feeling, letting go, and moving on). It is one of the signs that healing and resolution are occurring.

To maintain denial of abuse, we may have attached ourselves to religion as our only refuge and comfort. This may have helped us survive. It may also now be reinforcing a repression. Healthy religion walks hand in hand with healthy psychological work, which involves addressing, processing, and resolving our issues. It is not escaping into something that colludes with abuse or invalidates our experience. It cannot be like exorcism, which only gives us a release and does not address the original trauma or stay to work on the integration of the personality. This approach may even reinforce splitting, creating a new dissociation. Solace, like exorcism, disincarnates, but it does not reincarnate.

Finally, since abuses are negations of personal power, we ask ourselves if any of the beliefs listed below are recognizable in our present thought processes. Are any of them traceable to abuses from our religious past?

- I have no real power.

- I will never be able to face anything alone.

- What I need is out there, not at all in me.

- My feelings, my sexuality, my body, and my impulses are dangerous.

- I come second in everything.

- I cannot trust my inner voice.

- I am not allowed to have my own wishes and needs nor to fulfill them.

- I am selfish as long as I try to be independent.

- My purpose in life is to endure pain, not to be happy.

- I do not really know what to do, how to take care of myself, or what I really need.

Griefwork releases us so that new affirmations emerge:

- I have the power to face the losses and abuses of my past.

- I express my grief with the full range of my feelings.

- I trust that grace will transform my sadness into letting go, my anger into forgiveness, and my fear into love.

- I parent myself by allowing my feelings, letting go, and moving on.

- I am thankful for the grace that has helped me recover from my past and recover its riches.

- I have full permission to live in accord with my deepest needs and wishes, to say no to abuse and yes to happiness.

My joy is in the realization that my capacity to love remained intact no matter what happened to me.

Healthy community enterprises are aimed at serving individual wholeness. This means encouraging our lively energy to be released. Lively energy is our exuberance, our brightest enthusiasms, our imperishable passions, our irrepressibilities — what becomes our bliss. This energy is meant to open more and more in the course of life in the service of our deepest needs, values, and wishes. It makes us capable of giving joy to others. This is the very same elemental energy in the universe itself. It is what raises a storm at sea or erupts as a volcano. It shoots into the surprised sky as a sudden geyser. That is the same energy poised to rise in us. The only difference is that nature cannot be stopped but our energy can be inhibited or interrupted. Our Whee! can encounter a Whoa! instead of a Go for it!

"God and Nature bid the same," Milton says in Book VI of *Paradise Lost*. There is an organic unity between nature, human psychology, and spirituality. The link is this liveliness we see in nature. The awe of it is contact with archetypal forces of the universe that are personified as God and are made conscious by our human selves. A personal relationship to God means honoring the organic unity of ourselves, nature, and God. This happens when we are in touch with our liveliness. Nothing can annihilate it, but can only divert it. We can get it back at any time by our program of recovery: grieving the past, feeling our feelings about it, and letting go of it while preserving its riches.

Our lively energy makes us able to dare and to defy. Recovery from our religious past may mean defiance of its power over us in the present. Morality is not moral if it contradicts good psychological sense or the healthy inclinations of nature. Morality was never meant to interfere with the full activation of our human powers and possibilities. When we remain afraid to say no to violations of our liveliness, we are at the mercy of them and eventually even inflict them on ourselves. If we are afraid to laugh or weep or sing because of prohibitions, our lively energy is blunted and even dispelled. Once religion is recognized as a tool for liberation, withheld consent to life is the real sin.

Sex provides an example. It was meant to rise in adolescence as our personal participation in the life-giving exuberance of nature. Nature incarnated itself in us in an especially charged way in that period of life. Our only task was to learn to let that happen responsibly if others were to be involved. If the rules of the Church made any exploration of our bodies a mortal sin, we may have become afraid to see our bodies as a source of pleasure and release, and our lively energy was thereby squelched. A truly healthy adult would say no to such interference with nature's processes. Instead of quaking because of mortal sin, we might have laughed out loud when we were told it was wrong to masturbate and that any sexual pleasure willed outside marriage meant hell. We did not have it in us to say no to the hell on earth such injunctions meant for us. To recover is to have such a no in us now. It is never "so late to build in chaos" (*Paradise Lost*, Book VII).

Familiar Fears

An important step toward adult faith is confronting our religious fears. We fear what we have not integrated. In Catholicism, we inherited three religious distortions, and as distortions they could not be integrated. They are rejection of Christ's full humanity, which is the rejection of our own; rejection of the power and necessity of grace; and a tendency to view our bodies, our world, and sex with suspicion. These correspond to three specific heresies in the history of the Church: Monophysitism, Pelagianism, and Manicheism. Each of these exaggerated perspectives needs to be realigned in adult faith.

Part of the Church's sin (refusal to live out one's destiny) is slowness in any full upgrading in these three areas. We are responsible, as individuals of conscience, to reinstruct and reform ourselves. In our work of recovery, it will help to examine these raw places in our heritage, since they have so often led to dissatisfaction, confusion, and pain.

Fear of a Full Humanity

In the fifth and sixth centuries, the Monophysites in the Eastern Church challenged the Council of Chalcedon (451) by stating that Christ had a divine nature but not a human nature. This view was condemned, and the Eastern Church was then interdicted until 519. Though the official Church preserved the orthodox view *de jure*, we can see that throughout the ages prior to Vatican II, Christ was viewed *de facto* as divine to the detriment of his humanity. This reflects the neo-Platonic emphasis of St. Augustine on God as totally other.

The main deleterious effect was on spirituality, which came to be considered "disembodied" and "otherworldly." A prominent emphasis in the Church from St. Augustine (fourth century) to St. Alphonse (eighteenth century) was on freeing the soul from its imprisonment in the body. The glorified body of Christ (post-Resurrection) was considered our model and goal. Any mention of the physicality and sexuality of Jesus was noticeably missing in most spiritual writings.

This view is also antifeminist, because Christ as a model meant a male as a model. His choice of male apostles and the appointing of St. Peter as leader were thought to mean that the hierarchy and power structure of the Church were meant to be male also. This lopsided view of Christ as the male incarnation of God with no acknowledgment of how humanity includes both the male and female genders, inextricably united, makes the Incarnation a male event. "God became man" might well be taken literally as "God became male." Actually in the context of incarnation "man" means "human," not "male." Women have been barred from the priesthood because of this biased view.

Behind this is a fear of women's power and of nature's power. These fears are the results of centuries of refusal to accept the humanity of Christ as universally approbating our human and natural condition. The Incarnation honors humanness and earthly reality as most appropriate vehicles for the transcendent. Our transpersonal destiny can only be articulated, embodied, and completed in fully human terms. Yet, we have often feared our own humanness, seeing it as inherently wayward and untrustworthy.

True spirituality includes bodiliness, as Brother David Steindl-Rast says. Our bodies are not second-best in the spiritual life. They are the best and only vehicles we have to work with on our spiritual path — as well as on our psychological path. To see Christ only as the divine Pantocrator, the distant God, is a denial of the incarnation of Emmanuel, God-with-us, living a shared humanity.

> God's love could only fall upon the human heart, an object prepared from far and near by the nourishments of the earth.
> — PIERRE TEILHARD DE CHARDIN

The Discounting of Grace

Pelagius (355–425), a British monk, challenged St. Augustine on the issue of free will and predestination. He had some refreshing ideas, but his work was condemned as heretical in 431 by the Council of Ephesus. His main heterodox belief was that grace was unnecessary. People could be saved by their own will and effort. (We now understand that he viewed reason, understanding, and free will as forms of grace.) Grace refers to an infusion of power and discernment that exceeds the limits of our will and intellect. It cannot be created or won but is a free gift of God to humanity, that is, it is not generated by nature or ego but by a power beyond it.

The Church has aligned itself too often in history with official political power. It thus seems to act as if everything depended on human will and effort. There seems to be little trust in grace in the closing of the Jesuit missions in seventeenth-century South America to satisfy the slave trade interests of Spain and Portugal, in the Vatican Corcordat of 1933 between Hitler and Pope Pius XII, in the refusal of the American bishops in the 1960s to take a strong stand against the Vietnam War, in John Paul II's refusal to support the programs of Archbishop Romero in El Salvador, or today in the Church's refusal to support reasonable birth control or the right of women to all the sacraments. In effect, the institutional Church tends to make survival-of-the-establishment decisions. It is all too rare in history that the official Church has unequivocally trusted the Holy Spirit in open defiance of the political superstructure.

We all have a fear of trusting grace to come through for us. We inherited the distorted view that all that can be counted on is our own ego, cunning, and political machinations. Part of growing up in faith is recontacting the Holy Spirit within ourselves, that is, trusting the power of grace to pull us through — spiritually though not necessarily physically — as long as we act with integrity. The official Church may not help us do this: it may want to save its own skin, to protect its institutions, to maintain its status. Our own conscience and the example of present-day Christian models show us another path. We can trust a power higher than our ego accessible in the depths of our souls. We then find ourselves acting with consciousness, compassion, and truthfulness. This is the path from grace to effort.

Such trust in grace makes it easier to be witnesses in the world rather than colluders with it. This path may not safeguard our institutions or even our lives. It leads to no safety at all. We will have no foothold except the Gospel. At risk is everything except truth and vision, the only survival that matters when faith is real. The challenge of faith is always the acknowledgment of an unseen, enduring, and powerful reality behind and despite appearances to the contrary: "They call us poor and we are the richest of all, dying and behold, we live," St. Paul says. The Church is what is referred to in his epistles, a local community of committed people who are living in an ego-defying way.

Grace shows the full extent of our personal world. Events and people come along just in time to show us the path or assist us in traversing it. "Grace does not force us to enter another universe; it introduces us into an extension of our own universe.... Each of us is aureoled by an extension of our being that is as vast as the universe. What we are aware of is only the nucleus which is ourselves,... a whole which unfolds," writes Teilhard de Chardin.

Grace fulfills human nature. Our work is not enough; the endowments of our intellect and will are not enough. Since grace is intrinsic, not extrinsic, it is not an addition to our nature but a condition of its fulfillment. Graces are not gained by effort but are given along the path to those who stay on it. Grace does not replace freedom but fulfills it by releasing our greatest potential. In this sense, grace divinizes human existence.

In grace the ego is not destroyed but rather supplemented and transcended. Indeed, Karl Rahner says that grace is indistinguishable from the tendency in the human spirit to transcend ego desire, self-absorption, and fear. To commit ourselves to action is the work we do (implicitly a response of faith). This means acknowledging the power of grace and the transcendence of the inner life as alive on one continuum. No merit can induce grace, and yet it is ever available since God is always sustaining us and always creating us: creation is grace. Grace is the Self-communication of God. The archetype of this is Jesus Christ.

"If anyone thirst, let him come to me and drink." It is appropriate to thirst, to desire. It is a direction of the soul and a useful one when it leads to the discovery of the "living waters" within, the Self that contains us and slakes but never quenches because it is eternal.

> *What is above creation cannot be attained by action.*
> — *Upanishads*

The Faces of Dualism

A third-century Zoroastrian Persian, Mani, was the main importer of dualism to the West. St. Augustine was a Manichee in his early life but later repudiated the doctrine. The Manichees held that the body is evil and the soul good, a Platonic view that paralleled St. Augustine's own. Though Manicheism was condemned as heretical in the fifth century, its dualistic view of humanity reemerged throughout the Church's history with the Bogomils, Cathari, Albigensians, and Jansenists. Martin Luther was in this same tradition, as were John Calvin and John Knox.

Ever-recurrent dualisms spawned divisions between body and soul. Sex was looked upon with fear. Many saints taught hatred of the body. The Church became the conservatory and perpetrator of fear and taboo. Pleasure itself was considered sin if it was enjoyed or chosen. This attitude has continued in various forms from St. Augustine's time until the present. A frightened, narrow view of sex can create a hell on earth for sincerely pious people. The sign of an adult, responsible, and joyous Church is that it fosters happiness "on earth as it is in heaven." Discipline in healthy terms means not indulging the part of us that wants to be hard on ourselves. The warrior is vigilant and exercises continual custody over the archaic organizing principles that are life-negating.

The linear logical thinking of the scholastic philosophy of the thirteenth century has been the paradigm of Catholic theology until recent times. The Church's official stand on abortion, birth control, homosexuality, war, and many other issues, tends to reflect an adherence to a line of logic rather than a respect of nature's reality. The scholastic model is not based on honor of the human organism but on an imposition upon it of syllogistic thinking. Concept thereby dictates to reality. This is why the official moral stance of the Church continually requires upgrading if it is to be taken seriously by people who have found holistic perspectives in life. An adult believer today can confront dualism in the Church rather than simply reject it. The moral issue then becomes not whether but how behaviors and choices can become more and more responsible. This creates a context in which normal human behavior and morality are finally integrated (with considerable reduction of neurotic guilt!). A true moral law does not prescribe; it describes. It does not say how things should be but how they are.

Morality is a function of the human psyche, as old as humanity itself.
— CARL JUNG

The Virtue of a Larger Life

The accent in dualistic moral positioning is on fitting human versatility into categories. These may exist only on paper and do not necessarily honor the changing exigencies of individuals. But there is another reality, one that transcends logic and will: grace. Religion is the human response to grace through faith, ritual, belief, devotion, and virtuous moral living. That is the equivalent of union with God in the same way that virtue is the experience of likeness to Christ. It does not have to be formalized as membership in a parish. Community is an option but not a necessity. Moving in and then out for a while is a common style nowadays. Most of us will participate in a community for as long as it is respectful of our unique needs and leads us to greater consciousness of our spiritual path and our political and social challenges.

My thinking "I" can never be large enough a concept to encompass all that I am. Only when I is the universe, visible and invisible, does that happen. A larger life than that of ego animates us, and that life is the transcendent life of the Self. The life of grace as a participation in the divine nature is alluded to in 2 Peter 1:4. God wants our salvation, that is, that which is deepest in us wants our wholeness to happen. This is the same point that Emma Jung makes psychospiritually: "An inner wholeness presses its still unfulfilled claims upon us." The work is to cooperate with that exuberant and reliable drive and to allow it to have its way, that is, the Way. Carl Jung wrote to Sigmund Freud in 1910: "What infinite rapture and wantonness lie dormant in our religion. We must bring to fruition its hymn of love." A religious life is the marriage of heaven and earth. Heaven is wholeness. Earth is what we call home and the path to it. Religiously, we are like Dorothy asleep in Kansas and simultaneously en route to the Emerald City.

True religion makes us powerful. The religion of our past may have impinged itself upon us with attempts to prevent the emergence of our powers. Perhaps we wanted to flee its repressive or moralistic grip as soon as possible. But something in it may still touch us, and from that no escape is necessary. What endures in a touching way has endured because it is an ingredient that the psyche requires for wholeness. It is the invitation to individuation, the point at which healthy psychology meets and is blessed by religion.

Religious yearning persists in human beings. It has stood up to all the divisions and suffering that religions have brought. It is something uniquely cherished, intimately personal, not vulnerable to the shaming and repressions of any religious past. It emerges from the same sense of wonder and desire to share that made a hand draw an antelope on a cave wall. That yearning does not go away with discarded rosaries. It calls for attention all through our lives. We lose so much of our deepest self when we dismiss it as superstition or renounce it as puerile. Letting go of the past can open the door to something wonderful and powerful that knocks untiringly: "Behold I stand at the door and knock and if anyone will hear my voice and open the door to me, I will come in and sit with him and sup with him and he with me."

Our Capacity to Go beyond Appearances

Ulysses is the personification of our unquenchable thirst to live in this world and visit one beyond it. He wants to explore many earthly places, and yet he also wants to visit the Underworld. There seems to be an irrepressible capacity, ever alive in human nature, to transcend itself. This yearning in us shows itself in every wish to make good things last, in every attachment to what fascinates us, and in every search for something to hold on to. These are spiritual longings since they are aimed at that which endures beyond the limiting phases of time. Jung says that this yearning for the spiritual is as strong in us as the desire for sex.

Religion originates in our capacity and longing for transcendence. The word "transcendence" refers to that which lives beyond the limitations of ordinary consciousness. This does not mean that the transcendent has to be outside us. A higher power than ego can also be within us, that is, a vibrant and intuitively tuned inner life. This can be what is traditionally referred to as the indwelling of the Holy Spirit, a spiritual equivalent to an inner source of nurturance in a healthy adult. It is our essential being. In the Eastern view, it is Buddha mind. Transcendence is a way of affirming that a power greater than ego is at work within us, that is, the Self. Buddha nature is enlightened being as the being of all beings. The Self is the light of light.

At the same time, that which transcends us can also contain us. St. Paul says: "In him we move and have our being." Thus the transcendent is both that which makes us more than our ego and that in which we have our existence. Both these directions of the transcendent are ways of referring to the Self. Individuation is precisely this twofold but unified experience of the Self as within and beyond us: *I am more than I seem to be and something more than me upholds me.*

The sacred, or holy, is anything that partakes of the transcendent. The Self is the sacred. "Nature expresses something that transcends it," says Mircea Eliade. The sacred is not separate from us but is the deepest and ultimate reality of us and things. Once we see that nature and all that is has a transcendent dimension, the sacred becomes an affirmation that there is an expression of no inner and outer division in reality. All dichotomies end in such holy unity. The realization of the presence of the holy / sacred / transcendent and the realization of nonduality probably occurred to human beings in the same instant. Here is the actual instant in which it was grasped by a writer of the *Upanishads:* "This supreme unborn spirit of humankind, unaging and undying, is the same as the spirit of the universe, and this is the refuge from every fear." Tarry to contemplate and savor the richness of that statement!

A capacity for transcendence seems to be inherent in human nature. It is not simply an accretion of religion. Rudolf Otto, in his book *The Idea of the Holy,* says the experience of the sacred is founded in "an original and undeniable capacity of mind...independent of perception." Bernard Cooke expands on this in his *Sacrament and Sacramentality:* "Religion is best understood as both the quest for and the response to that which is truly ultimate. By ultimate we mean that which is fundamental to life, that which transcends the superficial world of provable fact, that which leads to some sense of a total order, a mooring, and a meaning. One way that people have expressed their religiousness is by describing an experience of what can be best identified as the holy — that profound sense that there is infinitely more to experience than we can explain. The word 'holy' points toward that which transcends or eludes comprehension, toward an awareness beyond our ordinary perceiving and conceiving. The word 'mystery' expresses a sense of ignorance deeper than that which can be dispelled by information." (Bernard Cooke, *Sacrament and Sacramentality,* p. 23)

Once we acknowledge the reality of a transcendent "higher power," there is no distinction between the merely natural and the totally supernatural. Everything is, as Karl Rahner concludes, a "supernatural existential." Implicit in concrete reality is the transcendent, something enduring behind fragile — and yet translucent — appearances. "The mode of God's immanence is transcendence," says Gregory Baum, who speaks of faith as "depth experiences": human events that consolidate meanings and render our mortal existence and our transcendent destiny one coherent continuity.

Traditional dualistic theology emphasized the gap between humanity, nature, and divinity, the wholly otherly quality in the divine. In a more expansive theological vision, the human contains the divine. We are human with a divine core, just as nature has a divine core. The divine life does not have to be restored by a savior but has to be realized by all of us, with many saviors and teachers to help us. This is what is meant by the shift from the outsider God to the insider God. It did not begin but was rather rediscovered in modern times. There were always sages (and heretics) who knew this truth. In the frightened and limited view of humans as merely rational animals, an elevation to divine life is required for wholeness. In the more open and trusting view, just being and acting in human ways is enough, since human includes heart and that heart is God.

We now can appreciate the deeper implications of the word "supernatural." It is manifested in those moments when the natural is honored as having a divine life. Everything is larger than it appears. The word "God" personifies transcendence, but not transcendence of humanity or of nature. God / the Self transcends ego; love transcends ego. This is what is meant by God is love. *There is no supernatural realm above the natural one, only an invisible realm within all visible things.* Once nature enters the divine equation and is recognized as having consciousness, "supernatural" becomes a word that describes nature's exalted state. Ken Wilber says: "Supernatural is simply the next *natural* step in overall or higher development and evolution."

The *Bhagavad Gita* says: "My higher nature is the life force that sustains the universe." The Christian theologian Origen added, centuries later: "Understand that thou art a little world and that the sun, moon, and stars are within thee." The first quotation shows the identity of humanity and divinity, the second of humanity and nature. Scientist Richard Plzak adds: "All matter is created out of some imperceptible substratum . . . not accurately described as material, since it uniformly fills all space and is undetectable by any observation. In a sense, it appears as nothingness — immaterial, undetectable, and omnipresent. But it is a peculiar form of nothingness, out of which all matter is created." Is not that no-thingness the God of the mystics, the Buddha mind, the Self?

Human nature and divine nature are two sides of a single coin. God present in us means there is something in us that dares us to transcend ego with all its arrogant boasts and its fretful limitations. Our positive shadow side refers to our unguessed and untapped potential. The cosmic spiritual potential of humanity *is* the divine life in us. When the limited ego takes its bow, the curtains open to a boundless possibility ready to make its appearance. Our darkness is a doorway to our unlived life. (Since practice is about dethroning ego, this is how the positive shadow is befriended by spiritual practice.)

Peter Berger, a Lutheran sociologist, in *A Rumor of Angels,* speaks of five "signals of transcendence." These are evidences in us that account for our belief in the transcendent. He lists:

- Our innate longing to find order in chaos

- Our playfulness

- Our indomitable hope

- Our outrage at evil

- Our irrepressible sense of humor.

I add the following:

- Our ability to go on loving no matter how we are treated by others

- The durability of our capacity to love no matter what happened to us in the past

- Our willingness to put ourselves second, even to risk our life for others

- Our capacity to forgive and let go, not to give up on people

- Our ineradicable belief that there is goodness and redemption in every human heart

- Our sense of accompaniment by a protecting presence

- Our knack for showing our best when things are at their worst

- Our intuition that reveals more than we logically know

- Our refusal to accept defeat in the face of unalterable odds

- Our discontent with what lies within our grasp and our consequent striving for what lies beyond our grasp (our inclination to stretch)

- Our power to say, do, or be something that leads to healing ourselves and others

- Our abiding sense that the universe is friendly and that there is a loving intent in all that happens to us.

In short, we have it in us to put love before survival, as the nursing infant smiling at his mother demonstrates when he thereby loses the nipple. We also have it in us to go beyond appearances. This is a way of saying that we have a transpersonal identity beyond our personal one: "Your names are written in heaven." Something in us keeps defying the facts at hand. We are more than the facts show or that our minds can know. We leap beyond limits, sometimes even beyond the conditions and limitations of human existence. "We taste fullness in the void, dawn in gloom, discovery in renunciation" as Karl Rahner says. We are more than we seem. The reality behind appearances that breaks through the conditions of mortality is the divine. We both see it and participate in it. "A rose is a rose is a rose" also means "a rose is more of a rose than ever we knew as I am more of a Self than I know."

The transcendent life in our psyche exists independently and yet is uniquely personal. The transpersonal dimension of ourselves is the other side of our own unique selves, that which transcends ego consciousness. It is a short step to see this as the ground of being, the spaciousness that underlies all reality, the Buddhist void, the mystics' God, the other side or rather the most deeply inside of us, the everything within reach. The deepest reach of inner wisdom is emptiness, the ground of all the archetypes. Jung calls this the "matrix mind," and it is same as the Buddha mind. Jung says: "What we call the dark background of consciousness is higher consciousness; thus our concept of the collective unconscious would be the European equivalent of Buddha — the enlightened mind." (Notice how all these expressions — inside, ground, space — are metaphors. We are not defining the divine but only attempting to approximate how it might exist with respect to us.)

The renaissance in art began with a realization that the essence of human existence is divinity. Our renaissance of faith happens when the transcendent breaks through into our quotidian reality and we begin to trust that it everywhere upholds us and yet nowhere secures us. The breakthrough, the experience, and the risk of trust in the midst of uncertainty are all the ways the personal ego enters an axis of power with the transpersonal Self. Wholeness is arrival at that axis. Joy is what it feels like since we are at last fulfilled.

> *...we are sure*
> *That beauty is a thing beyond the grave,*
> *That perfect, bright experience never falls*
> *To nothingness, and time will dim the moon*
> *Sooner than our full consummation here*
> *In this odd life will tarnish or pass away.*
> — D. H. LAWRENCE

T W O

Claiming Our Inheritance

*We are in grave danger of losing a spiritual heritage that has been
painfully accumulated by thousands of generations of saints and
contemplatives.... Above all, it is important that this element of
depth and integrity — this element of inner transcendent freedom — be kept intact as we grow toward full maturity.... We
are witnessing the growth of a truly universal consciousness in
the modern world.... To cling to one partial view ... and to treat
this as the ultimate answer to all questions is simply to ... make
oneself obdurate in error.*   — THOMAS MERTON

We have set ourselves the task of investigating our deepest spiritual
yearnings with a light from our religious past. This involves an ongoing
dialogue between psychology and religion as well as both Western and
Eastern spirituality. Our work is to distill what is truly catholic from
the layers and accretions of so many authoritative personalities and
cultures over time. The collective experience of humankind is the history of the human psyche and is sacred history. Our most basic need
to be human is described in that story. It entails a passover from the
limits of a scared, arrogant, or retaliatory ego to a generous Self of
love, wisdom, and healing power. The divine is the foundation, source,
and ultimate destiny of this paschal mystery. Jesus is the forerunner
and exemplar of it, as are Buddha and St. Francis. Every age provides
models of the virtues we are meant to practice.

Our Global Inheritance

Our full inheritance is that of all humanity, not just that of any single
religion. Nothing is "the one and only" in a mature approach to faith.
One creator is not enough. We are all continually creating, and everything is creating us. Elie Wiesel says: "There is no messiah, but there

are messianic *moments.*" One savior is not enough. There are many
redeemers in our human history. Jesus was one; Mohammed was one;
Buddha was one; Martin Luther King was one. Ntozake Shange in
A Daughter's Geography puts it this way: "We need a god who bleeds
now, whose wounds are not the end of anything."

What so often makes Christianity ineffectual in reaching out to the
pluralistic world is its insistence that Christ is the only Son of God, the
only Savior, the only way to truth. Such a limiting Christology does not
accommodate the vastness of the divine embrace. William Blake wrote:
"Jesus is the only God...and so am I and so are you." There has to
be room for endlessly multiple articulations of divinity in all of history
and in all cultures. There does not have to be a single God as Father in a
realm beyond the clouds. Every truly authentic fatherly moment in our
life is an experience of the fatherhood of God, every motherly moment,
of the motherhood of God, every loving moment, of the loving God.

It takes a whole village of spiritual ideas and practices to raise one
healthy, spiritually mature adult. Religious faith does not address all the
territories of the psyche that require cultivation. A truly cultured person in today's world cannot become accomplished with the resources of
only one hemisphere. West needs what East offers and vice versa. Religion needs psychology; psychology needs spiritual practices and vice
versa. Sincere religious persons know they cannot find all they need
in one religion but cull wisdom from all of them to round out their
parochial knowledge. Separatism is no longer sensible in a world like
ours. Our inheritance is not that of our family or of the religion of our
childhood but that of the world.

An informed Catholic today has looked into the Eastern vistas of
Buddhism and Taoism, the wisdom in Judaism and Islam, the theological perspectives of Protestantism. A good Catholic is as fearlessly
catholic as that. It works the same way for Buddhists and Mormons
with respect to Catholicism. We all need each other to design a full
and rich spiritual life. We keep hearing the same message from so
many sources, or rather from the one Source of archetypal wisdom
in the psyche of humankind. A catholic faith is one that respects the
illimitable breadth of revelation.

St. Clement of Alexandria acknowledged in his *Stromata* that Buddha had "extraordinary holiness." The Buddhist perspective helps us
through the conditions of existence in ways that cannot be found quite
so cogently in Western religious faith. At the same time, Buddhism is
not sufficient for a psyche as rich and varied as ours. We require the
ritual and the special history of wisdom residing in our own religious

tradition. Our rituals have contained our passages, granting us a sense of beginning and ending. We inhabit them and they uphold us.

The Dalai Lama was asked whether we should leave our religions and become Buddhists. He answered no and suggested instead that we maintain a continuity with our past while also integrating Buddhist perspectives into our present life. It is always *both ... and* not *either ... or* in mature discussions and intelligent decisions. Every source is the Source.

Trusting synchronicity (meaningful coincidence) involves trusting that our past figures into our personal destiny in some unique and useful way.* To be born a Catholic means that fact figures in how our personal destiny will be fulfilled, how our spiritual potential will be best accessed and activated. In fact, our religion is part of who we are and what makes us unique. It has values and truths that speak to us in personal terms, no matter how empty of meaning it may have become for us. It is crucial flora along the landscape of our path. Nothing in our life story was meant to be wasted or jettisoned. Spiritual evolution means continuity with our past and finding the riches in it, familiarly, culturally, educationally, and religiously. Disparagement of ancient mythic motifs deprives us of a living vision of our roots. Since Christian and Eastern archetypes and motifs are the same, disparagement of one repudiates the other.

The shadow side of the Church is in its stunting of our growth toward adulthood. The Church often controlled us with fear and threat. The most insidious way in which that hurt us was by foreclosing on our chances to discover and release the light that was in us. How do we reach our full stature? How do we release the spiritual potentials that lie hidden in us? It happens in two ways: we make continual choices for love instead of control and we are guided by those who do the same. We need teachers and guides who are motivated by love, not power.

Both Christ and Buddha have characteristics that speak to what is deepest in our personalities and in the archetypal psyche. They are fitting mediators between the material and the spiritual worlds. Both represented an immediate and simultaneous comprehension of evolution and destiny. Both enunciated an affirmation of an inner reliable coherence in time and in human events. When we are stirred by love that takes us beyond ego desire, our attraction is toward this effulgent unity.

---

*See my book *Unexpected Miracles: The Gift of Synchronicity and How to Open It* (New York: Crossroad, 1998).

To deny the value of oriental teachings is like having a compass that lacks east and yet insisting it is quite complete. Here are some examples of wisdom from the Eastern world that supplement and complement a Christian view:

• Yoga is a practice that leads to a union of what might separate or what has separated. It helps us recollect what has fragmented in our bodymind. There are a variety of types: Hatha Yoga has a physical focus; Raja Yoga is an intuitive meditation path; Jnana Yoga emphasizes reason and intellect to see through the illusions that arise when we are caught in addictive fear and desire; Bhakti Yoga stresses feeling, devotedness to a master and / or a path of devotion that shows us what to do when the love we feel is greater than our capacity to feel it.

• Eastern approaches suggest a spiritual practice that does not cling to forms, a spirit of nonpractice. This frees us from routine and rote and keeps reminding us of the noneffortful grace of spiritual progress. Mindfulness is the Eastern meditation and life practice that shows how to let go of the ego's tricks and to make direct contact with the present. Mindfulness is a refuge *in* the present, not away from it. The Holy Spirit is just such mindfulness, the pure energy of the divine life in this moment and place.

Chicks are born when the egg forms and reborn when the shell breaks. There is a Taoist saying: "The hen embraces her eggs, always interiorly listening." The warm energy heats only the shell, so she transmits more penetrating warmth through her mind. Even if she leaves the nest, she is alert to it as her center of attention. She conducts heat to the eggs wherever she is. Spiritual rebirth happens when we are warmed in both those ways. This metaphor refers to continuous attention from meditation pillow to world. That sitting place is always a center of gravity.

• Eastern thought emphasizes the combination of opposites and the continual transformations of evolution. "Living midnight" is a Taoist image signifying deep stillness that is nonetheless filled with the energy of the coming dawn. Midnight symbolizes the transit from serenity to activity; noon from activity to serenity. The stillness is the pivot of the spiritual life bringing us from the light to the light-needy world and back again. This concept echoes the tradition of mysticism in the West.

• The Buddhist path emphasizes the emptiness / spaciousness of the self and of all things. There is no solid, freestanding self nor is there a supreme Other with solidity. Eastern views are thus free of dualism, a characteristic of the Christian tradition as we inherited it. "The man of eternal renunciation is one who neither hates nor desires; beyond dualities, he is easily freed from bondage," says the *Bhagavad Gita*.

Evolution is a movement toward synthesis, not sameness. Catholics who want to be catholic can no longer afford to confine their life pilgrimage to the city of Rome. The whole world is ours and all the wisdom of all the traditions. It is time to wake up like Rip Van Winkle and let go of our royalist leanings. We are in a democracy now and have full access to all the wonderful riches of space and time, of cyberspace and no time at all, of psychology and science, of Buddha and Sufism, of every library and every word in any tongue that tells us where God is. If Christian faith is authentic, it will be able to remain intact after we find Buddha's truth and Mohammed's or anyone's. Truth stands up to truth. Nor do the truths of science dispute religious truth; they are companions of it. Every truth confirms the truth.

A single transreligious interior truth is articulated in history through many religions. Spiritual seeking means looking for an alignment of our inner archetypal truth and the truths in religious revelation. That is why any sincere search leads us back to our deepest selves. A true religion is not one that can trace its roots back to a single historical originator but one that has succeeded in preserving and mirroring the universal truth of the psyche.

For example, it is an inherent truth of the human psyche that goodness wants to keep giving its gifts to others. In Buddhism, this is articulated by a commitment to the Bodhisattva path. Bodhisattva means awakened warrior. Those on a spiritual path are warriors in the sense that it takes discipline to stay with their practice, to subordinate the ego to the Self. Bodhisattvas have reached Bodhicitta, the awakened mind, the wholeness of bodymind free of the fears and desires of ego. They are committed to six *paramitas* (virtues): generosity, discipline, patience, exertion, meditation, and knowledge. With this vow comes a spontaneous inclination to benefit others. The experience of wholeness releases an urgent yearning to share. The principle here is that we are wholly enlightened as individuals only when we are all enlightened as a human race. An enlightened person stays in the world and keeps returning to it out of compassion for all beings who need encouragement, teachings, and compassion.

In Catholicism, this same truth is articulated in the belief in the communion of saints, by which many saints in heaven continue to care about and pray for people on earth. The apparitions of Mary over the centuries and the images of her in the world particularly express this archetypal reality. Mary keeps returning to earth out of compassion for others. In this she is a Bodhisattva like the Buddhist Avalokitesh-vara, the feminine energy of loving kindness toward all beings that is continually reincarnating to serve the needs of humankind. How is this assisting presence manifest? The ways cannot be enumerated. Once our spiritual practices become part of the routine of our lives, they inhabit our world with us. This is one example of what is meant by being con-tinually surrounded by teachers, saints, and bodhisattvas. St. Therese is one: "I will spend my heaven doing good on earth."

The universal principle in the psyche that underlies this concept is that love keeps revisiting the beloved and that those who are enlight-ened want to share their gift. The archetypal theme keeps arising in all religious traditions since it addresses the very essence of who we are and how we evolve. It is found in philosophy too: Aristotle in the fourth century B.C. taught that goodness is always diffusing itself. It cannot remain inside; it overflows and has to give itself. Love is what goodness looks like when it is given away.

Love does what nature does: ever renew its gift no matter how un-worthy humankind may seem. The human soul is the world soul, the life force, one center of gravity. It is an irresistible and irrepressible directedness in all things toward fulfillment of its purpose. This force has the power to glean everything necessary from people, things, and events to make wholeness happen. It is the pentecostal spirit that sweeps us up, resolutely intent on leading us to our destiny. The life force is an immense goodness that loves to give itself with no possibility of subtrac-tion or division and with no necessity for addition. It keeps multiplying itself unstoppably, irresistibly, and uninterruptedly. Our own capacity for enthusiasm is an image of this. Enthusiasm means filled with the divine life force. That is the human and natural life force too. This is what is meant by our being made in the image of God.

Great saints and saviors did not achieve salvation / enlightenment and then break contact with us. "Behold I am with you all days," said Jesus on the day of his ascension from earth. In a hymn to Mary on the day of her assumption into heaven, St. John Chrysostom sings: "You went away but you never left us." The archetypal truth of the Bod-hisattva path has always been firmly present in Christian theology and in all religious traditions. To believe that only the Catholic articula-tion or only the Buddhist articulation is the right one is idolatry. It is mistaking the messenger for the message. It confuses personal psychic truth with personifications of it.

To find Buddhism or Catholicism as a path does not mean that it is the only one that can speak the truth but that it is the one that most adequately approximates our own psychic truth at this time in our lives. It is synchronicity, a meaningful coincidence between truth and a way of knowing it that fits for us personally. But no matter how exalted and incontrovertible it seems to us, it is still only the most recently appealing and most nearly accurate portrayal of a perennial truth. Such truth is immemorially known and continually restated throughout human history. The best attitude is gratitude and openness, not attachment and certitude. Fierce loyalty to one religious perspective may be another trick of the arrogant ego that insists that its choices and traditions are the only legitimate ones. To use another example, the psyche believes that death is not the end of the cycle of life but only part of it. Christians proclaim that with the image of an empty tomb, Hindus with reincarnation, Buddhists with rebirth. Yet the belief in enduring life is greater than any single enunciation of it. It is already and always a psychic fact deep inside us. It would be known even if no one ever said it.

A Universal Yearning

The work of reclaiming the riches of our faith thus begins in our own psyches. It then has recourse to our religious tradition. Finally, it looks into any other tradition that speaks to us in ways we can understand. When we find a cogent and touching way to integrate a universal truth into our life we have much to be thankful for. It is the manna in the wilderness, real but perhaps temporary, to those of us en route to a Promised Land that offers even more nourishment. Once we acknowledge we are beings on a path, we will never know if this is our final religious view or our final religious affiliation. What looks like a stop may be a step.

We can leave a church or abandon religious practices, but we cannot leave our psyche, which goes on proclaiming the same revelations that religions do. Something, we know not what or how, is always at work bringing the good news to life. Religions are mediums of an abiding and irrepressible message in the heart of humankind. Why would we want to give that up? It would be a betrayal of our deepest reality and our most reliable support.

"Under every shrine to Zeus there is an earlier altar," wrote Hilda Doolittle. My Italian grandmother spoke all her life of the church of her childhood in Meta di Sorrento: Our Lady of the Laurel. I went there as an adult and found that it was built on the ruins of a temple to Minerva. Our Lady of Guadalupe appeared at the very site where the goddess of the Aztecs had a temple, and she was wearing the goddess's colors, green and gold. There is an ever refreshed continuity of religious truth, ritual, belief, and devotion all through human history.

St. Augustine summed this up: "That which is called the Christian religion existed among the ancients and never ceased to exist from the beginning of humankind till the coming of Christ" (*De Vera Religione,* 10). St. Thomas was a student of the Arab scholar Averroes; Augustine learned from Plotinus and Plato; St. Albert the Great learned from Ibn Sina; Jesus based his teaching on the Hebrew scriptures; Teilhard de Chardin learned from Marx and Engels; Thomas Merton was a student of Buddhism. Great thinkers do not consider their own tradition sufficient. All find ways to integrate and expand their own traditions from the matrix of others. This syncretism is a quality of mature religious faith. It is how the continuity happens.

When the Church does not allow synthesis to emerge from thesis and antithesis, it ceases to be a living evolutionary system. Instead it is a container of styles and formulations of belief that become anachronistic. Trust in the Holy Spirit, that is, the animating and creative force of the divine life, means commitment to preserve truth through the permitting of diversity. There is no reason to fear diversity once we trust the holy spirit of the psyche, the mystical Self in all of us that can always find its way back to the truth — or rather into it.

There were always healthy traditions in Christianity that refused to let go of primordial images but built from and upon them: to the Teutonic people, the oak was associated with the god Wotan, who hanged himself as a willing savior on it. A tree is the Nordic symbol of the world. Wotan hung for nine days and nights, after which he was resurrected. St. Boniface, the apostle to Germany, cut down the sacred oak tree at Geismar that the pagan people were worshiping there. But he used the wood to build a Christian chapel to St. Peter. He did not destroy the past but renovated it. The tale of St. Boniface shows how the ruins of the past become building blocks for a richer life in the present — precisely the point of this book. Respect for ancestral images makes for a continuity between the best in their tradition and the perennial truth that is transtraditional. This is audible in these words from a sermon of St. Clement of Alexandria: "I will give you images to understand the mystery of the Logos."

Historically, the city of Rome has represented intolerance of differences. This happened politically in the building and maintaining of the Roman Empire, which exploited rather than cultivated the unique resources of other peoples. It happened religiously in the repression and persecution of "heretics" and "witches" during the Catholic Middle

Ages. Ancient Rome demanded that all nations capitulate to its will. In that sense it is like the grandiose ego. In religion Rome still wants authority over all: our body, soul, thought, and behavior. Mature religious faith demands that an individual say no to that oligarchic hegemony. Real faith is dialogue. Latin was the language of imperial Rome, which continually suppressed tribal cultures and dialects. In our time the change from "sacred" Latin to the vernacular was one of the first signs of the decline of "empire" and the acknowledging of our catholic destiny: to embrace all peoples and derive our powers from their varied riches. Roman should not be the opposite of catholic but part of it.

Truth is the hidden treasure of the psyche. It is mediated through myths that tell it in story form. True religion preserves and ritualizes it. When religion codifies truth and makes it into an orthodoxy, the mythic experience can be lost. Myths are not meant to be destroyed by religion but fulfilled by it. Religion does this as it invites us to reach higher levels of consciousness and grasp the divine-human meanings in myths. (Divine and human are on a continuum like psychic and religious truth.) Religion is both historical and transhistorical. A myth underlies the doctrines of Catholicism, and it is full of exuberance and truly good news. Archetypal gods were transformed into believer-friendly saints, and this led to devotion. Popular rituals were transformed into sacraments that celebrated the truths of rebirth and eternal return.

Religious images are both personifications and real. Real means reflecting a psychic truth. This combination of opposites is distasteful and incomprehensible to the ego. The logical mind does not permit any forays into the realm of the poetically real. This is why faith is necessary if we are to have a full experience of our interior life. What irony that we need to go out of our minds to find the deepest truths about ourselves!

Myths are parables about the dimensions and destiny of the human psyche. They are the first version of depth psychology. The sources of Greek myth are Homer and Hesiod. Xenophanes in 565 B.C. took issue with the anthropomorphism of Homer and Hesiod. "One god is highest...neither in form nor thought like mortals." The philosopher Thales proposed that gods existed everywhere, not just on Mount Olympus. Anaximander said that there were no gods. The psyche will not accept "no god." It always relocates divinity, no matter how lost or disavowed it becomes. Something in us knows there is more to us than intellect and will. Theagenes of Rhegium (525 B.C.) said that the names of gods represent human faculties or natural elements. The Stoics were also sophisticated and proposed allegorical interpretations of myths. Chrysippus in the first century A.D. said that gods are physical or ethical principles. By the end of antiquity, no cultured person took myths literally. The psyche triumphed in freeing itself from literalism (idolatry) while still maintaining its belief in divinity. That is what is meant by reclaiming the riches of the psyche and religion.

The work of adult faith has always been to retrieve the old images from their personified forms and bring them back home to reflect the truths of our inner life. To reclaim our religious riches is nothing less than finding ourselves. In other words, the images behind the dogmas are ours, and our work is to recover them and restore them to our psyche, not in the "nothing but" way but in a "both...and" way. Timeless truths keep reappearing in history. Ancient voices enunciate today's intuition. Ulysses at Epiris asked the dead for guidance. This is a parable: something from our past, from our origins, is still helpful and still alive and we can contact it. This it is I-in-communion, the communion of saints, the Bodhisattvas of all the ages.

Truth is discovered in time. This means that timing is essential to the process of finding the hidden treasure. Padmasambhava, the mystic who brought Buddhism to Tibet in the eighth century, hid some of the deeper spiritual teachings in scrolls in various caves in the Himalayas. He trusted that they would be found when people were ready for them.

Is my gloom after all the shade of his hand outstretched caressingly.... All that thy child's mistake fancies as lost I have stored for thee at home.   — FRANCIS THOMPSON

Finding the Riches Within

In 1922, after long and arduous excavations, Howard Carter peered for the first time, deep under the ground, into the tomb of King Tutankhamen. His friend, Lord Carnarvon, called down to him and asked, "What do you see?" "Wonderful things," he responded after a breathless pause.

Archetypal Catholicism is more expansive and appealing than fundamentalist Catholicism. We can preserve the archetypal riches while no longer adhering to the dogmatic formulations. This safeguards and evokes the riches of the past without being bound by atavistic views that may violate the living reality of perennial wisdom teachings. We may no longer be Catholics who swallow dogmas whole. We may be Catholics who live in the wholeness of an archetypal faith.

Images that have lasted through the centuries recommend themselves to our attention. Part of adult faith is looking for the mythic meanings in religious beliefs, especially those that are common to universal traditions: incarnation, resurrection, community, and the sacraments that invite us to participate in these mysteries. Our long work in searching out the tunnels, caves, and holes in our religious past leads us to the treasure chamber, the mythic images of our own destiny, to "wonderful things." Once we look past the organizational trappings and traps, we locate a special room, shut up and lost for so many chapters of our life. In that room are heirlooms that waited for us all these years.

These treasures are the archetypal meanings that underlie the beliefs and rituals of our religion. They reveal the mystery of the transcendent and show us how to access the graces of it. The main way to reclaim the archetypal riches in our childhood beliefs is to see them as living metaphors. We each find our own way to these interior meanings and a relevance for our life in the present. Metaphors are not only literary but descriptive of the depth of human / divine being.

God is a metaphor that beckons us to the mystery of the Self in all its transcendence. It does this in three main ways: Something in us and beyond us is greater than our ego. To speak of God is to acknowledge grace, a power of the Self that supplements and completes our ego. Something in us and beyond us transcends the conditions of our time-bound existence. Rooted in the impermanence of all that appeals to us in the world is the potential for our enlightenment. Something in us and beyond us transcends nature and all its wonders. God is a way of saying there is something behind appearances that is not limited by them, something in the ever reviving cycles of nature that endures and that continually supports us. In other words, God is the metaphor for the mystery of transcendence. This mystery proclaims and promises what *we* are: we are more than we seem; we have more love than we have ever shown; we are bearers of infinite light and of letting it through; we have an identity in a realm beyond the one we see.

Enlightenment is an accurate grasp of reality as unalterably tied to the conditions of existence and transformatively tied to release from any fear of them. This happens through a sense of the interconnectedness of all things, and this is why compassion is always the characteristic of the awakened state. This is sanctity, the Western word for enlightened compassion. A saint is any one of us who reinvents the divine life in our own lifetime. The heart of God becomes thereby a human heart. A caring love arises in us for those still lost and dazed in the sunset of fear and ego-centeredness.

Mircea Eliade, in his book *Myth and Reality,* shows how great religious myths embody and enshrine humanity's deepest realizations about its identity and its destiny: "Myths are a constant reminder that grand events took place on earth and that this 'glorious past' is partly recoverable. . . . Rites [of religion] force man to transcend his limitations and to take his place with the gods and mythical heroes so that he can perform their deeds." "He who believes in me shall do the works I do" (John 14:12).

Gregory Baum, in *Religion and Alienation,* says that "idolatry is absolutizing the finite and elevating a part to a whole." There are two extremes. Taking teachings literally is idolatrous. Taking them as merely metaphorical in the literary sense is reductionist. Somewhere between these is an archetypal richness that has an authentic foundation in the human psyche and in the reality of the felt world. The richness is not reached through an analyzing intellect, which will insist on choosing *either* literal and *or* metaphorical. It is reached by contact. It is a participatory experience. It happens at the soul level, where conscious and unconscious meet and opposites reconcile. "The spirit does not dwell in concepts but in deeds and facts," says Jung. For instance, the Incarnation can be seen as a metaphorical way of acknowledging that supreme love becomes real only when it appears in human beings acting it out in history.

Here is another example: The stations of the cross are familiar from our childhood. They may seem maudlin or inordinately focused on the gruesome details of Christ's sufferings. But as a metaphor they walk us through the steps of the letting go of our ego. They detail how it has to accept the weight of the world's unfairness, how it finds few people willing to join in bearing it, how it is has to be nailed down in full self-denudation, how it has to hang suspended and helpless, how it has to be buried and lie in silence. These are stations on the way to resurrection: the steps to the awakening of the enlightened Self. The wisdom of the ages was always right there around us in the Church, waiting to be acknowledged in its depth dimension. To do that is to wake us to adult faith.

The *heart dimension* of the faith discovery is precisely this luminous transit we make from ego to Self, from fear to love, from powerlessness to power. Unconditional love is in and is the True Self, the archetypal "God within," its center everywhere, its circumference nowhere. The Sermon on the Mount describes unconditional love in practical terms. It spells out exactly how the grandiose, narcissistic ego can be transcended. Real faith always leads to love, and love is only possible when

ego enters its service. In the Sermon on the Mount, Jesus spares no
hide-out or disguise of ego in his razor-sharp delineation of what love
means: "Do good to those who hate you, love those who hurt you,
bless those who persecute you."

True faith is a gong of generous love, not a tinkling cymbal of distinctions. There is a Sufi saying, "Generosity means doing justice without
first requiring justice." Every religious tradition has the same recom-
mendations as Christ's Sermon on the Mount. All through the ages
there has been a living tradition of nonviolence and generous love.
Every religion has produced saints who have kept this tradition alive.

Some of us learned of a God made in the image of human ego, one
with an unalterable insistence on punishment and reward. The ego gods
are primitive and ungenerous. The identity Jesus reveals is love, not fear.
A life-enhancing adult faith is one that shows, brings, exemplifies, and
teaches the egoless and fearless love that Jesus lived. This is how he is
divine and how we share in divinity. The statement of Jesus "I have
overcome the world" means the Self has overcome the ego. Frances
Wickes wrote, "The Self can be the most difficult and perilous of all
possessions, as it was to Jesus. It can lead to crucifixion of all that the
ego has held most dear."

The engendering of fear in us has been the worst patrimony of organized religion. We were afraid of our bodies, of our free thought,
of our instincts, of our passion, of our own potential. To recover the
riches of our heritage requires a transformation (salvation) of the ego,
caught in fear and desire, to a Self that is free of fear and desire. It is
a grace and a task, received by grace and achieved by faithwork, our
spiritual practice in the context of religion. The Sermon on the Mount
tells the ego how to let go of its arrogance and its impoverishment. It
does this by proposing:

- Reconciliation and forgiveness

- Nonviolence in disputes

- Example, not coercion

- Generosity

- Returning good for evil, blessing for curse, love for hate, and
  compassion for hurt

- A value system that respects love and wisdom over position and
  wealth

- Letting go of anxiety about how things will turn out

- Letting go of judgment and competitiveness

- Banishing the three witches of self-distrust, self-denial, and self-disgust.

- Seeing hate as a form of suffering and negativity as not yet having a useful view or finding skillful means.

These principles represent wholeness in human living because they are ways of loving. They are steps in the dismantling of the arrogant ego and the granting of strength and choice to the impoverished, victimized ego. Morality for an adult means exactly this kind of perfection. This means no longer being under the influence of fear or neediness. It is true psychological sobriety and wholeness. It is conscious work that transforms the self-defeating habits of ego. Psychological adulthood means building a healthy ego, one that is functional, that is, works to bring us to our goal of effective and happy living and relating. At the same time, our psychological work is to let go of the neurotic ego with its insistence on control and entitlement, qualities that prevent us from effective and happy living and relating. (The Sermon on the Mount is the recipe for this.)

Our spiritual work thus mirrors our psychological work. In both, we increase healthy ego skills and dissolve unhealthy ego attachments. Our natural ability to scheme and be tricky is a humbling appearance of our shadow side. Ego and its capacity for limitation and mean-spiritedness reveal us to ourselves, as Iago kept learning. Spiritual practice has as its goal not enlightenment but the state of being in which our *first reaction* to others is not from our ego mind but from the heart of Christ, the Buddha mind, our higher Self. Thus the ego's automatic reaction of conditional love can become unconditional love; ego biases can become expansive and generous wisdom; retaliation can vanish into reconciliation. Our first impulse is not to get back at but to get back with. Through practice that new set of responses becomes habitual. That habit is called sanctity.

Morality is thus an actualized capacity for goodness and love, a spiritual means to a spiritual purpose. This is the equivalent of healthy functioning in our psychological life. Spiritually, we are functional as we move toward our destiny of love, wisdom, and healing. Adult morality is meant to perfect our psychological work. The old adage of theology "Morality is the quality of a human act" can now be restated: Morality is the perfection of healthy acts, the holiness of wholeness.

Here are some affirmations of the moral transformations implicit in the Sermon on the Mount. As with all affirmations, they support rather than replace active, visible, behavioral change. It may be helpful to notice which ones ring a bell for you. Write out and say (as often as you choose throughout the day) the ones that strike you.

I am the rightful heir to all the earth has to give.
I accept the conditions of existence.
I release more and more mercy into my world.
The universe is benevolent to me.
I am pure of heart and see God.
I make peace and am a child of God.
I acknowledge pain and persecution as part of life.
I let go of the need to punish or to take revenge.
I let go of the need to get back at anyone.
I let go of the need to get even with anyone.
I let go of the need to correct others' impressions of me.
I choose reconciliation.
I let go of my grudges.
I let go of the need to be right or to be justified.
I admit when I am wrong and apologize.
I let go of stubbornness and rigidity.
I let go of the need to control others.
I am comfortable with power.
I let go of perfectionism; I am perfect as I am.
I drop the need to be the center of attention.
I am open to criticism and feedback.
I look for what is true and build on it.
I look for the good and praise it.
I appreciate myself and take care of myself.
I release myself from shame, guilt, and self-blame.
I choose gentleness in all my affairs.
I let go of my belief in the effectiveness of violence.
I let go of the use or praise of violence.
I drop the use of put-downs, insults, or sarcasm.
I love those who hate me.
I bless those who curse me.
I do good to those who hurt me.
I help others care for themselves.
I let go of anxiety about survival and security.
I let go of judging others.

I am always on the way to the light.
I let the light through.
I release, love, wisdom, and healing into the universe and receive
    it here and now in my life and relationships.

*At every point in our lives we are called to conversion.... We
are radically unfinished yet filled with stunning grace. Our
personhood is oriented to completions that are received, not
achieved.... Religion encourages us to reach out to the mystery of being, indeed to the mystery of being more than our
present self.... Donating ourselves presupposes self-possession.
... Psychological and spiritual health [means] that we continually
enlarge the images by which we understand ourselves.*

                              — WILKIE AU, S.J.

Catholic means universal consciousness, universal humanity, and
universal love. Evolution is about how God consciousness becomes
physically alive in the world and in us. In that sense, evolution is incarnation. Our part is to allow it, to salute it, and to risk it. This means
having a life purpose that is not oriented toward a goal of acquisition,
ego advancement, or safety from the conditions of existence. Our life
purpose in the spiritual world is not a goal but a glory. It is a passionate
intensity about our world and an arousal to action because of our love
for it. Nature fills us with pleasure to encourage procreation. Grace
encourages its own evolution by filling us with joy when we find our
life purpose and pursue it.

    Our religious journey begins in a parish, a useful and necessary point
of origin. A parish is meant to be the local embodiment of a universal
love and faith. We may lament the narrowness or inhibition we suf-
fered in a Church without such consciousness, but our wounds can be
openings through which we all locate and enter a new world, the one
in which Catholic means universal love. A devout Catholic is one who
is engaged zealously in taking us all into that kingdom.

    The ego world is local; the world of the Self is catholic. Each needs
the other if incarnation is to happen. It has taken this millennium for the
inclusion of all of us in the incarnation of Christ, and we are inheritors.
For the next millennium we are pioneers, and what awaits us is surely
crucifixion and resurrection, the completion of the Christ's majestic
work. Real faith is readiness, without excuse or escape, for the life of
Christ to become our own in every detail.

    These ideas are not yet in all catechisms, but they have always been
in the inner catechism. Our inner voice, our divine interiority, the God

within is a trustworthy authority. That makes us brave enough to be
Self-governed. We feel the joy that is natural to us as free beings who
know our names as they are written in heaven. That joy was lost to us
by our succumbing to fear and parochial defensiveness. The Lamb of
God who takes away those sins is granting us the peace that is always
and already ours.

THREE

Paths to Faith

Spirituality is letting go of a self-absorbed ego in favor of universal love and wisdom. The ego will not give itself up. Only grace makes that happen. To allow such letting go takes faith in grace, something unseen and uncertain. Thus everyone on a spiritual path has faith. Religion is a relationship to the divine life beyond ego. Religion activates spirituality by morality, coherent beliefs, ritual, and devotion.

Bonds That Last

Most of us began our life of faith in childhood. We were introduced to beliefs and to a community of believers. We may thereby have formed a durable bond to the Church. This bond was established before we could say no to it. Childhood indoctrination usually results in a yes without the ability to say no. It is not an informed consent, but a blind obedience to authority or family. This religious bond can go on uninterruptedly, even when we reject childhood beliefs or membership in a church. It is beyond personal control or choice. This is why it is not real faith, which is free and consciously chosen and rechosen. Adult faith is a yes when we are free to say no. However, this enduring bond to religion can always be the foundation of a spiritual path or can make a contribution to it. Whatever remains alive in our psyche does so because it can contribute in some way some day. We are given a lifetime to find out how.

A lasting bond that is not existentially renewed in the here and now may be called an essential bond. It is like the essential bond in an intimate relationship. We are bonded in a longstanding love for one another, in a history together, and in a connection to one another. All these qualities can be present while a couple is getting a divorce. For a relationship to work, these unconditional qualities have to be balanced by existential — here and now — conditions of love and commitment shown in action. The essential bond requires an existential commitment to make a living bond.

This is a metaphor for religious bonds. We may have an unconditional, even unnoticed bond to our childhood religion, but to be real, it has to be complemented by an existential commitment. Here are three examples of essential bonds:

The Bond of Memory: This is a remembered sense of warmth, belonging, and security. It is usually based on "how good it feels" to be in church or at religious rituals. This bond is responsive to images, words, fragrances, and tastes. It is comforting and sense-oriented, granting a refuge from the demanding conditions of existence or from our own life predicaments. Such consolation may become an avoidance of direct confrontation with our personal challenges and responsibilities. Usually, it is simply "feeling good" with little effect on our life decisions. This is why it is insufficient as a full religious experience.

The Bond of Superstition: This is an attachment to beliefs and fears that remains in us below the level of rationality. It accounts for a continuing sense of guilt and shame, usually with a repertory of ritual behaviors that are meant to diffuse it. This bond is based on how scary the world is and how crucial it is to know the techniques that make it safe. It is the bond of moralism and legalism. "I have to wear this medal or else." Abraham Maslow describes this bond: "Most people lose or forget the subjectively religious experience, and redefine religion as a set of habits, behaviors, dogmas, and forms which at the extreme becomes entirely legalistic and bureaucratic, conventional, empty, and in the truest meaning of the word, antireligious."

The Bond of Experience: This bond is founded on a personal experience of the transcendent, a sense of a personal relationship with Christ or God. Such a bond can exist without personifications like God or Christ and can be oriented to the higher Self. This bond can occur within a believing community or individually. It can refer to one experience that was powerful and unforgettable, to a series of experiences, or to a long-lasting continuum of experience.

All three bonds are connected to the four elements of religion — belief, morality, ritual, and devotion — but not necessarily in mature ways. Most of us have all three of these bonds operating in us, though the first and second may be most in evidence. For instance, we may not have gone to church in years, yet when we are thrown off-balance in a crisis, we feel the need to pray or to visit a church. This may be a signal that the bond of memory of our religious past still rekindles a consoling sense of safety, something we feel good going back to.

We may find ourselves feeling guilty about a harmless pleasure, proscribed in our religious past. We may light a candle at a shrine for a relative who is in danger of death. These reactions may signal the bond of superstition. (Lighting candles prayerfully is an age-old, legitimate ritual that becomes a superstition when we believe it works magically, that is, that it obliges God to respond.)

Finally, we may have an abiding or sudden sense of the presence of the divine in the silent woods or at the birth of a child. This may be a sign of the bond of experience. A mature personal bond to Jesus means having his heart in us, a heart of courage for our journey and of love for other beings on their journey: I have a personal relationship with God not only because I talk to God but because I act like God and for God in this world. I am the way God feeds the hungry, clothes the naked, comforts the afflicted. In this bond, Christ may be a personification of the eternal Self summoning me to tell my life story with love.

Any essential bond, either of memory, superstition, or relationship, links us to the Church of our past, but it may not sustain a life of faith in the present. That happens only when the essential bond is joined to an existential commitment: a living, day-to-day responsiveness to the life and teachings of Christ or to his values. This is what is meant by putting faith into practice. An existential commitment is an ongoing life history of personal choices to live the divine life in one's here-and-now existence. The essential bond is formed in the past; the existential commitment is renewed in the present. The essential bond is a given; the existential commitment is a choice. Considering all three bonds, an existential commitment is most likely to happen in the context of the essential bond of experience.

As we saw above, a person may leave the Church and still notice the presence of an essential bond many years later. This is not faith but a historical vestige of connection to the Church. At the same time, a person can leave the Church and still make life decisions that center around the Gospel message. This shows faith without active Church membership. Likewise, one can remain in the Church all one's life with an essential bond of memory or superstition with no existential commitment ever fulfilling it.

The challenge is to acknowledge the kinds of bonds we hold. Then we may choose to form or solidify a bond of experience that becomes translated into existential committedness to a life of faith-in-action. True faith combines receiving and committing. We receive a message, form a bond, and then commit ourselves to live in accord with the message in a community of faith or on own.

Some of us carry around antiquated images of faith and the Church. We imagine that these archaic models and beliefs accurately represent the present Church. But our models may be anachronisms, half-truths, or even beliefs the Church once held but no longer holds in the same way. One of the first issues for adults who choose to examine their faith is to distinguish between the images and recollections of childhood belief and the living message of faith in its most intelligible and intelligent representation now.

What Is Faith?

"Faith," according to Richard McBrien in *Catholicism,* can be defined as "personal knowledge of God gained through the experience of God (revelation), mediated by a community of faith," and "belief is an expression of faith." Thus faith is not simply cognitive but heartfelt. It is not the opposite of experience but directly related to it.

Once one has faith in God, one believes that faith itself is a gift of God. It is not of human making nor can it be produced by effort. It comes by grace received, not achieved. Faith happens only beyond what the mind can conjure. It transcends the limits of ego and intellect. At the same time faith seeks understanding. We keep exploring faith and belief to grow in appreciation of its depth and meaning. This helps faith evolve but does not create or increase it. It remains a part of the gift dimension of life waiting to be opened. The Kabbalah says: "He who reaches out is reached." "Within reach" is a promise.

Faith leaves room for free choice since it offers no incontrovertible evidence. Nothing about it is absolute or perfectly clear. Scientific knowledge is based on predictable, repeatable, ineluctable evidence. One has to assent. Faith is beyond that which is scientifically provable. Thus faith is itself a bravely transcendent act because it leaps beyond reason. Faith is not belief without evidence but conviction with no need for evidence. True faith combines all human opposites and thus even includes doubt. Faith is a life-span reality, evolving as we evolve, sometimes by regular progress, sometimes by a quantum leap, sometimes by a long silence, and sometimes by a crisis of confidence and doubt.

There is an analogy between faith and art. Paul Klee, the Swiss artist, said: "Art does not render the visible, it renders visible." A thing is truly and fully seen only in its artistic form. Art presents, makes present, the inner life of things. Faith creates this same vision, the vision of the inner life of things beyond the phenomena, the Rose beyond the rose, the Self beyond the ego, the divine beyond the mortal appearances.

There is also a personal and community dimension in faith. This does not have to entail membership in a church. We can act with compassion and love in solidarity with our fellow humans whether or not we are co-members of an institution. In other words, faith is real within a church community or within the human community. What matters most is that it is personal, interpersonal, and transpersonal: it represents a personal commitment within an interpersonal context for a transpersonal purpose. Where our compassion begins God begins, where our compassion ends, God ends.

Adult faith does not mean simply holding on to the consoling images of the past as we do in the bond of memory. That may feel like faith but may be only loyalty. Here is an example. Transubstantiation does not have to refer to a transformation of bread and wine into the divinity of Christ; it can also refer to a transubstantiation of humanity into its divine identity. We, however, may *need* to believe in the traditional formulation of Christ's presence in the Eucharist because it is so consoling. The Real Presence gives us a reliable security when we are sitting quietly in a church and see the red candle burning. Even after losing faith, we can be holding on to what worked and still works in the sense that it still has the power to comfort. A poignant example of this appears in the book and film *The Lonely Passion of Judith Hearn*. Judith has "lost" her faith, and while looking at her familiar picture of the Sacred Heart, she says: "Is this the only You there is?" When the picture is on the mantel she adds that it makes her feel so at home.

Icons and images fill our lives with archetypal significance. The archetype of the father becomes the God above with the white beard. The archetype of the mother becomes the Virgin Mary. A friend of mine once referred to St. Maria Goretti as St. Maria Alberghetti. She confused two icons from her childhood: a saint and a movie idol, Anna Maria Alberghetti. When I pointed out the confusion of the two names, she said: "Wasn't it all the same to us, the distant virginal females who were so beautiful and who were supposed to be our models while at the same time being unattainable?" So much of our childhood faith was indeed an attempt to contact the archetypal sources in our psyches. Religion served to introduce us to a transcendent world meant to be within us yet presented as unattainable. The adult task of faith is to recover the connection.

Throughout history at least three perspectives of faith in God have obtained:

1. God is a personification of a mystery that defies conceptualization. In this approach, God is a metaphor for a transpersonal mystery, not the mystery itself but a vehicle to it. If the metaphor is symbolic only in the literary sense, faith does not seem to be present. For example, Euhemeros (300 B.C.) said: "The gods are *only* reflections of our own human nature." This is a reduction that nullifies the reality of the transcendent Self beyond ego. On the other hand, a living metaphor is one that affirms this underlying reality. Jungian, Eastern, and mystical perspectives fit here.

2. God is the person of the mystery, the mystery in person. In this approach God is not a metaphor but a person. One can stop here with no need for religion, or one can be a member of a believing community. This is deism, faith in a personal God that may not include beliefs, moral positions, rituals, or devotion.

3. The personal God reveals himself and reveals a way to live here and now and to go on living hereafter by participation in the mystery, mediated through membership in a faith community and its rituals. When the mystery includes the Incarnation and Resurrection of Jesus Christ, the response is Christian faith. When that response is congruent with action it is faith in action. The Church is a community of believers who participate in sacraments and are beckoned to love and service. The Second Vatican Council added two emphases: faith is a free gift that invites a free acceptance, and Christian faith exists in Christians whether or not they are within the Catholic tradition: "All those who are led by the Spirit of God are children of God" (Rom. 8:14). This is faith in the traditional Catholic sense.

To believe is to approach reality with confidence in a loving power beyond earthly limits. "A believer interprets reality and human existence as finally worthwhile, intelligible, and purposeful," says Richard McBrien. Faith is a heightened capacity for perceiving what lies behind appearances and the connectedness of it (and us) all with a sense of awe and wonder. From this sense comes ritual and morality. Around it gather beliefs. Thus all of religion composes itself from faith.

The lowest common denominator of human faith is the acknowledging of a reality that transcends human power and human limitation. Hence faith is oriented toward a higher power: something more than human intelligence can contain and having more power than human will can encompass. Nicholas of Cusa, in the fifteenth century, quoting earlier mystics said, "God is a mystery whose center is everywhere and whose circumference is nowhere." "Center everywhere" means immanence (in me). "Circumference nowhere" means transcendence (beyond me).

If faith is a journey, any approach to it that is phase-appropriate makes sense. We may first believe in God literally and later as a metaphor of the higher Self of all humanity. The first three kings in the Old Testament, Saul, David, and Solomon, exemplify three dimensions of faith development. Saul lives in fear of the literal God; David has devotion to a personal God; Solomon sees God less literally and evolves a humanistic faith.

Religious metaphors in this book are not about comparisons but about the deeper reality of ourselves. A living metaphor is an experience, not just a literary device. It identifies and deepens reality. Actually, every metaphor is about the psyche. For instance, "March comes in like a lion and goes out like a lamb," seems to express only the weather conditions of the month of March. Yet, it is also about a human style of evolution. The inflated ego enters the world with force and then may be humbled and become more gentle. Some men go into relationships like lions and, as their egos get their comeuppance, they soften and become more sensitive. What seems a trite literary device is a living portrait of how the human organism is made. It follows that there is a spiritual meaning too: the lion lies down with the lamb.

We see an apple tree in early spring and believe that it has the potential of bearing fruit in the fall. Trusting potential requires faith; knowledge is not yet possible. We know that persons have actual skills and capacities that they use every day. We believe that persons have potential capacities that are far greater than any they might be demonstrating in a particular moment. The positive capacities of the higher Self — love, wisdom, and healing — were lived by gods and saints. They are personifications of these powers of the Self made actual. They are also personifications of powers that are potential in us. We admire reconciliation and generosity in the saints as possibilities in ourselves that are visible in them. We even know we can imitate such goodness and that is a source of hope. Virtue — like retaliation — is, after all, imitation. That twofold human possibility is always facing us imitators.

Now the meaning of faith becomes richer. Our faith is actually directed toward the potential glories of humanity and of nature. This is why faith is such a necessary feature of spirituality. It fosters Self-actualization. Belief in potential is a leap toward realization of it. In this sense, faith is a pathway to a fully inhabited life.

Ego is capacity for light; Self is the light. The target of faith is light, explicit in Self, potential in ego. Our faith is in the power of the light to illuminate our hearts with its love, our minds with its wisdom, and our bodies with its healing. When Emerson says: "So nigh is grandeur unto our dust," he is making a faith statement.

Faith is limited and stunted when it is about the facticity of historical events. It actually refers to the archetypal meaning of historic moments in which a divine potential became actual. Faith is not in believing, for instance, that the dead body of Jesus was revivified. To believe in the Resurrection is to believe that the death-resurrection cycle is a continuing and reliable experience for all of us. This happens when we consciously suffer a crucifixion of ego and love lives on. This is a faith experience. It may seem as if this approach to faith — and for that matter the intrapsychic view of the divine also — is too ego-absorbed. On the contrary, it is ego-expanding since it acknowledges ego's destiny of union with the Self. Faith is belief that there are cycles and that they are a track to such union.

Faith events are exuberant explications of the full potentials of our humanness. This is rightly called unthinkable. It can only be experienced *with* faith. Faith is not an alternative to experience; it supplements it. This follows from our evolutionary condition as humans. We are always in process, never all done. This is why we always need faith and experience, moving concomitantly and continuously.

And what is that experience? It is mindfulness: discrete or continuous moments of freedom from the ego's habits of fear and division. It is presence in the here and now without engaging in the mind's usual habits of distraction from them. It is having only one refuge: the Self, also called the Buddha mind or Christ consciousness. Then our first reaction to anything is love, wisdom, and healing. In other words, we are saints.

Authentic religion does not impose itself on us from without; it assists us from within. Once it is perceived as intrapsychic it is no longer alien but intimate. William James understood that the unconscious acts so powerfully that it can feel like divine influence. Theology, with its fear of psychological reductionism, distinguishes religious experience from psychic events. But, as we have seen, all religious experience originates and takes place in the human psyche. There is no division, only distinction, what Huston Smith calls "bridges instead of as barriers." The psychic event of appreciating transcendence or suddenly seeing it as a white light or as a homeless woman is a religious event because it peeks behind the most common appearances for a more profound reality. Now we glimpse the luminous meaning in these words of St. Augustine's fifteenth epistle: "The paschal mystery [death and resurrection] is accomplished in its interior and highest meaning in the human heart [interiorly]."

Conditions and Miracles

The Greek word *pistis* is a form of the Hebrew word for faith: *aman,* which means to become secure. This security is in God as the ultimate source of trust and meaning. Without faith, the conditions of exis-tence — transitoriness, pain, unfairness, death — are final, and life is a cruel joke. With faith, they yield to an ultimate meaning: an immor-tality behind the appearances of mortality. Adult faith is not an escape from the reality of human conditions but a realization that they are not the whole picture. They are only the figures that are backed by a ground of spiritual reality, as the ego is supported by the Self.

Christian faith looks behind impermanence and suffering to a ground of enduring life. Rotation and alternation, not polarity and dualism, express this life. The rhythms of dying and rising are not dichotomies. They imply one another, that is, they exist entirely in mu-tuality. The Resurrection did not cancel death but is implied in death. The mystery is not an empty tomb but a combination of opposites, death and life. Behind the figures of dualism, institutionalism, fear, and ego is the ground of reconciling and healing love enacted by us every time we refuse to give up on love. The risen Christ is the Self that endures and abides in us.

Faith is tested when we are confronted with apparent contradic-tions. In Luke 24, the two disciples en route to Emmaus lament that Christ was supposed to set Israel free from the Romans but instead he was defeated and his work destroyed. Jesus answers: "Was it not ordained that the Christ should suffer and so enter into his glory?" This response is an assertion of the paradoxical nature of the spiritual vision. The figure of death recedes to ground and the figure of new life emerges from the ground of apparent unalterability. Faith defies the facts at hand. Faith means seeing an alternate world, where nature's laws do not have to be obeyed. Paradox is the link between the figure we focus on and the ground behind it that we miss. Jesus' apparent defeat is really victory. In the marriage of opposites that characterize faith, one is implied and promised in the other. In the same way, the disciples' apparent loneliness is really communion with him. The Every-thing that they thought was lost is within reach and will break bread with them. It is spiritually significant that this revelation occurred when they were hopeless. It is often from within the void that we hear and see in a new way, another example of how a condition of existence can become a source of new life. Hopelessness, that is, the bankruptcy of the ego's expectations, is the condition most suitable to awakening. The reason the void can become so fertile is that it is the very spaciousness that is the ground of all being, the divine essence behind appearances, the space taken by the ego we see through and let go of once we awaken.

"Your faith has saved you" (Matt. 9:22) is a repeated phrase of Jesus that shows how faith has the power to create conditions on earth as they are in heaven. He did not ask for faith in miracles but used miracles as signs of the arrival of a transcendent kingdom. *Miracles are moments in which nature bows to transcendent possibilities.* Bernie Siegel says: "A miracle is an alteration in the direction and flow of creation." A miracle is an inexplicable phenomenon that gives faith more conviction. It is not a proof since proof is in the realm of logic and faith happens at a higher level of knowing. It is the arrival of something more than the ego thought possible, something that has happened against all odds. It is not that nature's laws do not hold up but they are suspended to reveal for an instant something that is always the case in the world of the Self, a law-transcending power. Miracles invite faith and evoke it, but they do not form the basis of it. They are not proofs but witnessings that manifest to faith from faith. They do not produce knowledge but enrich belief.

Thoughts are not held to the limits of time and space as the body is so why would grace be limited either? Miracles happen interiorly (for example, as inspiration and intuition) or exteriorly (for example, as healings of the body). Miracles are articulations of grace at work in the world of mind and nature. This grace motivates and assists us, but then we take over with ongoing effort. Grace shows us that the destiny we are headed for is not the ego's making, that wholeness is not owed to us.

Miracles are ultimately metaphors of inner possibilities. They are parables about the higher consciousness that overcomes death and limitation. They show there is something more afoot in the human story than the story. According to Samuel Taylor Coleridge, to suspend disbelief for the purpose of understanding the magnitude of the otherworldly dimension of something is poetic faith. Poetic faith sustains belief in that which is behind appearances. Some beliefs based on Bible stories are actually forms of poetic faith: Joshua making the sun stand still, the garden of Eden, hell.

Only dedicated hard work, not miracles, leads to lasting change in us. They are a flash in the pan, signs that more is needed than effort but not that less effort is required. St. Teresa referred to her own miraculous ecstasy not as *arrobamiento* (rapture) but as *abobamiento* (joke)!

Believing Is Seeing

Truth is within ourselves; it takes no rise from outward things,
Whatever you may believe
There is an inmost center in us all,
Where truth abides in fullness
…and to know
Rather consists in opening out a way
Whence the imprisoned splendor may escape,
Than in effecting entry for a light
Supposed to be without.

— ROBERT BROWNING

The reduction of religion to a simply scientific or psychological construct does the psyche a disservice. Inner certitude can happen intuitively in us without logic or proofs. Truth is anything that contributes to a coherent sense of Self and shows the reality of something more that lives behind limited appearances. It is meaningfulness that is personally, intuitively, and affectively validated. In the film *Contact,* we see how a truth can be experienced but not explained or proved. Faith is the word for that way of knowing.

The religious quest for meaning enhances us because it widens our consciousness and frees us from the limits of a purely rational or egocentric view of the universe and ourselves. The best about our potential as spiritual beings cannot be proven by empirical observation, that is, we cannot verify by experiment that it is predictable and repeatable. The task is to find our own meanings and then commit ourselves to actualizing and fulfilling them. This means being wholehearted while not necessarily certain. To find our meaning *is* to find an objective meaning once we see the validity of psychic reality. Buddhism helps us see that there is no freestanding, inherently independent reality in the universe or in us. This is how faith *is* the path.

The foundation of faith is surrender to ultimate meaning, not to demonstrable fact. Faith draws us into the transcendent mystery of our own and the world's existence. It is necessary for the full range of our knowledge of appearances and what lies beyond them. No single science or combination of all sciences (including noetic and extrasensory ones) adequately expresses the variety and depth of reality. Faith posits that there is a reality that transcends fact, proof, nature's ordinances, and sensory cognition. It is neither objective nor subjective but transcendent. It proclaims that reality is richer than science or intuition can contain.

A fundamentalist believes Christ rose from the dead in the sense that his inanimate, dead body was animated with new life. A nonbeliever says this never happened. Neither one of these statements is about faith. The former posits belief in a palpable and intelligible event; the latter denies that such an event occurred. Both base their view on whether or not the original event actually happened in a material sense. If the "believer" found out that the event did not literally occur, the believer would no longer believe. If the atheist found out and accepted that the event did occur, the atheist would believe. In both instances, the perceived authenticity of an event joins with one's acceptance of it to create belief or disbelief. In both instances, the inner assent is founded on the linear historical actuality of a fact. This is scientific knowledge, not faith, because it is based on proof of an ontological reality. So much of our Catholic past was about proving we were right or that mysteries were not really mysterious. We may have missed out on the wonderful dimensions of psyche and soul and how they can be stirred by their potential for divine wisdom and divine surprise.

"I do not believe in God" may mean I do not believe in the personification of God or this personification of God.

As a whole person, I accommodate many ways of knowing, not only the one that is based on provable, incontrovertible fact:

- I know you have money because I see the cash. *Knowledge through proof has led to certitude.*

- I know George Washington was the first president because I trust the records of history even though I cannot prove it as easily as I can prove that the doctor's credential is real. *Knowledge through acceptance of historical tradition with no thorough chance at proof has led to certitude.*

- I know my son loves me because I feel it, but I cannot prove it. *Knowledge through experience with no possibility of scientific proof has led to certitude.*

When I attempt to know the Resurrection in any of these three ways, I may be looking for (1) a certitude based on a physical proof, or (2) trust in tradition, or (3) personal memorable experience. But faith transcends all these and posits another element: an inner sense or knowledge that is self-validating. I believe because I believe. It is true because it is true. There is an analogy in Jung's approach to dream images. He says that they are not symbols of something beyond themselves. They refer to themselves. They are self-validating. They stand for and proclaim their own deepest meaning.

If something were to have to be real in the sense of the physical actuality of an event in order for us to believe it, then we would have the antithesis of faith. It is the same as saying "I won't believe unless I see and put my fingers in the wounds." I will not believe unless it is proven true: I will not believe unless it does not require faith! The scientific provability of the original events in Jesus' life is relevant only to those who cannot surrender their attachment to logic and proof. "The only way to live is like the rose without a why," as Meister Eckhart says. Further, St. Paul never mentions any event or miracle of Jesus. Christ consciousness is not about that man who lived in Galilee and all his wonders. It is about us and the shape and challenge of our capacity for divine life.

Actually, the certitude of faith coexists with a defiance of the way things are known in the linear world. It is not that the events of faith are ambiguous; it is that they are *more* knowable than any rational or intuitive mode of knowing can accommodate. They take place in sacred time and space (unlimited), no longer in secular time and space (limited). They are spiritual events, not merely physical events. The realm of faith is not the realm of news headlines but of an altogether new and mysterious way things happen. Faith is an untutored leap into an unknown reality. It is an initiation, not a logical conclusion.

"I can't be a Christian because I can't believe Christ rose from the dead in any miraculous way." Faith, however, is not about how Christ was reanimated from death to life but about how an altogether different way of living happened to him and how that is possible for us too. The fact of resurrection is the fact of a new way of being alive, not a reversal of a physical condition. We are in another dimension unknown to the mind. That is the mystery.

Death happens when the body can no longer carry the life force. Then, in the spiritual perspective, the student-soul goes home while her old schoolhouse crumbles. The mysteries of death and resurrection (rebirth) were celebrated solemnly in pre-Christian and early Christian times at Eleusis in Greece. The initiates maintained secrecy about the climactic, transformative moment of the sacred rites when ordinary death became the life that never dies. They did this because they were bound to it by promise. But there are two more reasons. First, one could only know by participation in the experience. So a noninitiate could not grasp the reality even if it were explained. Second, the initiates knew what was occurring only at the moment in which it occurred. Initiates did not know anything they could later tell!

Such an initiation refers directly to faith. It is an initiation into a way of knowing that cannot be defined in the usual way. Faith brings us into a reality, for example, the Resurrection, that did not happen in the usual way. It is known only by assent since there is no paradigm for it in the intellect. If one was standing guard at the tomb when this event occurred and saw it, one would still need faith. A Roman guard could not know the Resurrection any better than a present-day believer knows it. Its validity has nothing whatsoever to do with what one saw or could prove. The Resurrection appearance stories all have in common the faith of the respondents. Even though they saw, they knew by faith, that is, they discovered a new way of knowing at the same instant that they discovered Christ had a new way of being alive. The historic event was the bridge to a transhistorical meaning, known and knowable only by faith. Even words like "alive" are only metaphors for a mystery beyond our capacity to comprehend.

This same principle operates with respect to Christ's presence in the Eucharist. In a laboratory, the host is still bread. But it has a *sacramental reality* that is immeasurable and invisible to the naked eye and to the microscope. The sacramental reality is visible to the eye of faith. Faith in the presence of Christ in the Eucharist is based on a change in the *kind* of reality. Faith not only posits a transformation but even a new way of being real, one that transcends and defies linear objective science. It is not fact in the measurable historical sense; it is fact in the immeasurable historic sense. ("Historical," as used here, refers to what happened; "historic" refers to the significance of what happened.) To believe in the Real Presence is to believe that Christ is really present because there is a way of being present (sacramentally) that is more real than physical presence. The laws of science and nature are not acceded to here. To believe is to posit another mode of being, not just another way of knowing.

Faith is retired and canceled, not supported by proof. Faith is about *another way of being real*. The risen Christ and the eucharistic presence of Christ represent new ways of being real. The assent of faith is to this other reality that transcends finite being and beings. It is the immortal Self. Something is alive beyond the merely living. Living things die; the new kind of life does not end in death but ends death. This is why faith is so courageous. It never disparages reality but insists on expanding it. It dares to know another universe that is beyond but also within this one: "a compound nature, as a sod espouse a violet," as Emily Dickinson said.

Phases of Faith

Christ said, "You have not chosen me, but I have chosen you." Our arrival at or return to faith is not a choice first; it is a grace first, something that happens to us. It is beyond our own making, our own planning, our own effort. It is another example of the mysterious dimension beyond the grasp of the mind and yet assented to in the soul. We receive something and then we choose to act on it.

The existential choice to act in accord with the gift is faithwork: putting faith into practice. (Attention and fidelity to the inner world without external actions also can make a contribution if that is our style and calling.) We treat our gift with care by informing ourselves about theological and moral perspectives. It means self-discipline at times. It means learning and studying. It means living in accord with the lofty standards of the Sermon on the Mount. It is making Christ-centered choices. It is commitment to articulating in our every moment (all we have) the timeless love we gaze at in Jesus' heart (all we need).

We receive an inner gift only when we are ready to act on it. This is synchronicity, that is, meaningful coincidence of inner and/or outer events. Jonah refused his prophetic gift and soon learned there was no escaping it. But St. Augustine said, "Lord, make me pure, but not yet," and received some extra time. A free gift means permission for a free response.

It takes a long series of steps and shifts to reach self-realization. The old view that all is known and grasped in a childhood catechism is gone. We now see that our religious life is more like an evolving itinerary than a static grasp of universal truths. This does not represent a turning away from the spiritual; it is a profound respect for it. It is a recognition that the spiritual journey motif mirrors human processes of transformation: we find ourselves always evolving, changing, and growing in appreciation of truth, yet never quite possessing it.

The hero's journey story is encouraging to faith since it allows for a period away from religion as part of the process of truly finding it. The journey generally is described as having three phases, which apply to relationships, family, and careers also:

- *Containment* in the beliefs, habits, values, and behaviors of one's past. This is the phase of security.

- *Departure* from this womb-like structure to enter the world outside with all its challenges, dangers, and self-confrontations. The so-called "loss of faith" is a legitimate, though not universal, part of the process of growing up in faith. This is the phase of doubt.

- *Return* to one's roots with newfound powers: expanded consciousness, greater appreciation of the depth of original archetypal faith, flexible rather than rigid ways of loving and believing. The story of the prodigal son contains the archetype of what seemed lost but was always there waiting for us. This is the stage of returning to reclaim the wealth.

We may experience the consolation of belonging and then the alienation of rejecting en route to the integration of rediscovering. We respect our timing in each of these stages, neither rushing to the next one nor shamed for the current one.

In the first phase we swallow the teachings whole, that is, uncritically and literally. We look for boundaries to be set by others since we have none of our own. We project moral authority onto others, not yet ready to trust our own consciences. (Boa constrictors swallow their prey whole without chewing. They then cannot move but have to sleep for months while digestion happens!) Second, we set clear boundaries and establish our own identity over against the teachings of others (departure and struggle). Finally, we find a way to integrate our identity with the teachings (reunion and commitment). In each phase, we may begin with no clear boundaries, then set rigid boundaries, then maintain our own boundaries and honor others' boundaries. We are first closely attached, then strongly detached, then united comfortably.

Attachment: Childhood, Church as Parent

>   Blind faith: accept without question

>   Swallowing beliefs and moral injunctions whole

>   Guilt about what we have done; shame for being who we are

>   Obedience

>   No critical sense or boundaries

Detachment: Adolescence and Young Adulthood,
Church as Antagonist

    Doubting: struggle with questions

    "Picking and choosing" beliefs or moral standards

    Less guilt

    More struggle and rebellion

    Experimentation outside the accepted norms

Integration: Adult Faith, Church as Supportive Community

    Reclaiming archetypal riches and values

    Attention but not necessarily obedience

    Appreciation of and commitment to faith in a way that integrates spirituality and psychological maturity

Faith is thus a continuity of phases. Faith does not have to mean finding our final resting place in unaltering certitude or in any one phase. This would not be faith but fixation. True faith mirrors life; it keeps moving onward, a heroic journey, an evolution from light to dark and back to light. In John 14 we read: "Unless I go the Advocate will not come." In the fullness of the faith experience, one god-image gives way to another — a death to new life experience. A lively inner experience of full faith happens when the old containers of faith vanish and new perspectives and challenges arise and are greeted with courage and joy. Yet faith exists on a spectrum. The full experience is not the only one.

To move from phase to phase makes for normal development.

To be fixated in the attachment phase makes for regression or fanaticism.

To be fixated in the detachment phase makes for problems with authority and / or alienation.

We are just as much persons of faith, for instance, when we struggle as when we integrate. Even the undiscerning blind faith of childhood has its place in at least focusing us on the transcendent. The struggle is actually a life-long process and coexists with the other two phases. We may question even when we swallow whole; we question when we feel full faith. When we are angry or bitter, we are still in the struggle phase. As long as we are attempting to prove or convince, we are still struggling. As long as we are wrestling with faith questions, we are still struggling. Struggle and doubt do not signify lack of faith. They show the versatile nature of faith and its living quality of evolution. Only when we land on flat-line matter-of-factness are we through with faith: atheism with no interest in further exploration and total indifference to God or faith or religion.

The acceptance without question happens for most of us in childhood. The struggle happens in adolescence and adulthood and may include a period of rejection of faith. If we return to an appreciation of the archetypal and moral values of our religious past, though not necessarily to membership in a church, our journey is still complete. We have followed the heroic motif of containment, struggle-oriented departure, and reunion.

Faith also moves through stages like these:

Stage One: This is the stage of literalism, a one-dimensional view in which God is anthropomorphic and mirrors the human ego for better or for worse. The foundation for such faith is objective historical realities. This can be narrow and rigid in the face of the unruly conditions of existence. It is an uncritical assent. The accent is on reliability of authority and blind assent to the rules and dogmas of authority. The loyalty is to the institution rather than to individual inquiry. This is a dependent style but may be all that some people can handle; it has to have a place in a free catholic Church.

Stage Two: The symbolic and abstract take more prominence. There is a personal entry into issues, a greater internal motivation, a commitment to apply personal experience to the design of conscience. Here there may be a crisis of faith and more ambiguity. This believer is more skeptical and counterdependent but also has a place in the Church.

Stage Three: A more intuitive approach arises. There is more acceptance of paradox and mystery. One can recognize meanings and riches in what was rejected before. The mystery of unity of all things begins to dawn. This unity is about community and is interdependent.

It is impossible to understand or be understood by people too far behind or ahead of us in these stages so dialogue is difficult. We can only dialogue fully with those at our stage or who remember the one we are in or are headed for the next one.

Faith means meeting a subject — ourselves in God — rather than finding an object. There is no object after all, since the source of spiritual longing and the goal of it are one and the same. We are always and already in contact with the divine nucleus of our psyche and of our universe. It is the Self within us that includes and is yet beyond our ego: "its center everywhere, its circumference nowhere."

Institutions

Some people involved in the underground are eagerly looking for the perfect human community. They long for a community which fulfills all their needs. . . . This search is illusory, especially in our own day when to be human means to participate in several communities and to remain critical in regard to all of them. The longing desire for the warm and understanding total community is the search for the good mother, which is bound to end in disappointment and heartbreak. There are no good mothers and fathers; there is only the divine mystery summoning and freeing us to grow up. — GREGORY BAUM

In ancient Dodona, an oak was revered as an oracle by the local people. Later, when it became famous, it was dubbed an oracle of Zeus by the people and then even by the priests. Still later, what was at first a personal encounter with the tree became off-limits to the public and could be approached only by intermediary priests. This is a paradigm of what can happen to humankind's religious instinct. What begins as a personal encounter with nature and a reality behind its appearances is acknowledged as transcendent. Then it falls into the hands of a priestly class who decide how its graces will be dispensed. A living Church is not the guard of the sacred oak but the guardian of the peoples' right to revere it. The "it" is our inner psyche, nature, and God, all one experience understood from diverse perspectives.

To participate in a church community formally means to join in with others, who, like oneself, believe that the Church is *semper reformanda,* always ready, willing, and able to be reformed. To love a community is to accept that they and we are not perfect. Some reform is possible; some acceptance and coping is inevitable. Of course, we ask the Church to change as we ask ourselves to change. These happen together every step of the way.

Accepting the conditions of existence helps us to acknowledge that all human beings make mistakes, cause pain to themselves and others, close themselves off from feelings, fear change. At the same time human beings have a wonderful and irrepressible capacity for reform, for seeing the light, for learning to listen. The Church has this capacity, just as each of us does individually. Adult faith requires our confrontation of what is unhealthy in the Church and what calls for reform. To remain in the Church as a blindly obedient adherent is not an adult choice. An adult in faith is a member of an intervention team, not part of a denial system. This intervention team awaits us in some parishes. Part of the challenge is locating such team consciousness within communities of believers.

Institutions are best confronted by the solidarity of a group rather than by isolated individuals. We cannot fix the Church but we can confront its need to fix itself. We cannot shoulder the griefs of the Church, only our own personal experience within it. It also follows that the Church as community can ask us for the same acceptance "all the way to the bottom" that we give to and ask of any human beings we love. The work is, after all, interdependent and interactive. Nathaniel Hawthorne wrote: "We cannot deny our brotherliness even with the guiltiest."

We can, however, refuse to be false to ourselves ever again, insisting on a Church that accepts us fully, irrespective of our ideas, choices, gender, sexual orientation, or journey phase. A Church can validate and support us. It does not have to judge, condemn, and isolate us. Adults know how to recognize when a Church does or does not respect personal boundaries. They know just how long to fight, just how long to stay, just when to go. These decisions will not be based on our history or on a sense of loyalty or on sentimental nostalgic attachments but on what works for us now or in the long run. "What works for us" means that which confronts us on our deficiencies and that which is open to our confrontations of its deficiencies: a Church that speaks *and* listens.

The expression "fight from the inside" makes sense only when one is truly inside. To be truly an insider in the Church (or in any institution) means more than mere membership or participation. It means being inside the structure as a person with power. It is not enough to include oneself in the Church; one must also be included by the Church. "To make a difference from within" entails having a franchise, sharing authority and responsibility. To be able to work from inside we have to be allowed to be inside.

Robert Bellah defines the Church as "a congregational body bound in communion and conversation by an all-reconciling love." The love of Christ is the love we join in when we reconcile in ourselves the unreformed, reformable, and reforming Church. It will always be all three, another "given" — this time of all institutions. The Church, like all persons and groups, will always only approximate its own meaning.

The Second Vatican Council chose the title "People of God" in preference to "institution" as a title for the Church. Avery Dulles has proposed five major models: institution, mystical communion, sacrament of Christ, herald of the Gospel, and servant of the world. All these models coexist though the institutional model has tended to predominate in post–early Church history.

Many of us have an inborn mistrust of institutions. It is easy to think of ourselves in opposition to institutions. We forget that institutions are contexts for growth. They provide the security of order in which we have room to try our wings and rights to explore our options. They sometimes place stops in our way, but they also often create steps. This is how the human character develops: through both steps and stops. Our work is to grow in spite of their obstructions and to change them constructively so that they can serve our and others' needs.

In *The Good Society*, Robert Bellah says:

> it is hard for us to think of institutions as affording the necessary context within which we become individuals; of institutions as not just restraining but enabling us; of institutions not as an arena of hostility within which our character is tested but as an indispensable source from which character is formed. This is in part because some of our institutions have indeed grown out of control and beyond our comprehension. But the answer is to change them, for it is illusory to imagine that we can escape them.

Avery Dulles distinguishes between an institution and "institutionalism." An institution is an ordered society that works within a structure of hierarchy and regulations to fulfill a specific set of goals. "By institutionalism we mean a system in which the institutional element is treated as primary.... A Christian believer may energetically oppose institutionalism and still be very much committed to the Church as institution." An institution is a means to an end. The goal is sufficient order so that one can live and work serenely. Healthy institutions create limits on individuals. These limits protect the freedom of all. Institutionalism makes the institution an end in itself. Its purpose is to preserve itself at any cost. Its limits inhibit freedom. Person becomes secondary to system.

Institutions are a condition of humanity's world. The issue in faithwork is to identify how institutionalism has served us and how it has impinged upon our sensibilities and freedoms. To be a believer or church member does not require the waiving of even one of our human rights. We seek and can have a Church at the door of which we do not have to check our minds. We require not indoctrination but relief from ignorance. Blind faith is an obstacle to this. A purely rational faith will fade out as knowledge increases. Only an experiential faith survives the human growth process. An appreciative critique fits that kind of faith.

Yet ultimately commitment to any church will entail commitment to an institution. Even small faith communities gradually become institutional. In fact, even two people joined in marriage become an institution! As noted above, institutions provide a setting in which goals can be achieved. They facilitate movement, dialogue, and change. They help us confront our identity as one-with-many.

Institutionalism happens when the means is confused with the end. An institution bends itself and its habits to fit its ultimate goal. It does not become tied to a single formulation of the truth. It sees itself as a servant of its members. It continually reformulates, redesigns, and reorganizes to keep pace with changing times and needs. It acknowledges every model it may espouse as temporary and discardable in favor of one that is now more fitting. It sees the times change and yet can be trusted to conserve the timeless in the midst of every vicissitude. "The forms of Buddhism must change so that the essence of Buddhism can remain unchanged. This essence consists of living principles that cannot bear any specific formulation," says Thich Nhat Hanh.

Human connections are experienced both generically and specifically: I am in the Smith family generically, but as the third child, I have a unique experience that differs from that of my older brother. When the group is also international, I have a generic experience that is cross-cultural, one that is national, and one that is specific. Thus an American Catholic recognizes the Mass in Rwanda but may not feel fully at home in the ways the people participate in it. Each of us has a generic and a specific, unique, personal experience of our religion. No two believers are alike in their belief, and all are alike in some way. That is the only way human experience happens. It is not a problem, only a built-in given. This is why a spectrum of beliefs is legitimate and, when encouraged, leads to creative reexaminations of traditional doctrines.

One of the reasons the good news is good is because it includes us all. What we may have been exposed to in Catholicism was not the kerygma — a living, universal, limit-transcending wisdom — but a narrow, male-dominated, fear-driven, and shame-based antihuman burden: "This thing that hath a code but not a core," to use Ezra Pound's words.

The central criterion about whether institutions are human is this: can dialogue and support happen there? True Christ-like authority in the Church is stewardship: service not control. There was immense regional diversity in the early Christian *churches*. A highly centralized Church will have difficulty providing that. Adult trust in our teachers is based on noticing that their motivation is to put us in contact with our own inner sources and that they are trying to do the same thing themselves. We trust those who are not motivated by ego, not trying to control us but to release us.

William James warned of "faith in someone else's faith." We distinguish personal experience from what is experienced by others and handed to us as mandatory. We all have the privilege of doing what Giordano Bruno, Teilhard de Chardin, and Meister Eckhart did: come up with our own synthesis. This is part of the work of faith. An adult faith is designed by the individual in the context of the community but not limited by it if it is stuck in atavistic or life-denying beliefs. St. Thomas, Ivan Illich, Thomas Merton, and many more show the way.

Both traditional and modern views are useful in designing an adult faith. Tradition is not just the Church's historically common practice and belief. It is something handed down in our psyches too. There is a living tradition in our interior world. Within this inner world is a truth that transcends any single designation of it. We inherit from a vast treasury of faith preserved in all religions. Some of it has been forgotten by the community we live in. It is a great gift to the Church when someone remembers what has been forgotten and brings it to light again. When an institution can make room for such re-collections of faith, it is a truly living organism. The mind cannot reach the heart of the mystery of the Self. Faith is the supplement, as necessary as grace is to effort or imagination is to appreciating a truth. Faith takes us beyond our powers. It is a grace beyond the ego's resources. Our archetypal vision never contradicts true revelation, only the ego's version of it.

At the same time, there is no legitimate distinction between the Church as the "spotless bride of Christ" and the Church as this historical institution. The Church on earth is both bride and institution, sometimes stainless, sometimes sullied, always one single reformable congregation. The members of the institution are mainly responsible for confronting institutionalism when and where it creeps in. It is well-nigh impossible to accomplish this in a vast monolithic structure if one stands alone. But it is very possible when it happens as part of a grassroots communal thrust. It is a feature of psychological adulthood to reject the martyr position in favor of a cooperative commitment to make changes that serve everyone. The key word here will be "caring." To care is to love something or someone or some community enough to question, confront, and coax it to change. When caring persons meet with resistance, they find like-minded companions and together they persevere in the creation and continuation of dialogue.

Faith becomes a community event and churches are formed because good news cannot be kept to itself. The work is to be both a witness and a follower: "It happened to me so I bear witness to the truth of it." The Church is any place where one joins other witnesses. It is also the place where the glad tidings of our capacity for universal love are honored and are enlisted in the service of others both in and out of the believing community. The growth in moral adulthood that results is personal progress and contributes to the evolution of the entire human community.

There is definitely a move toward new religious structures in America today. The traditional religious forms may not appeal to liberals, but liberal churches are arising among people with higher educations and of higher economic and social class. At the same time, conservatism is growing, and one in five Americans call themselves evangelical Christians. Among both conservatives and liberals many are disaffected with institutionalized religion and seek smaller, mutually supportive communities of faith. Some individuals feel no need for mediators and believe they can have a direct experience of the divine. This is an ancient belief and quest in the human psyche. Inclusion of Eastern religious views and practices and membership in Eastern religions grew strongly in America and Europe in the 1990s. Disillusionment with traditional religion has led some to a search for the universal oneness offered in Hinduism, Buddhism, and Taoism.

The decline in patriotic and civil ceremony has also added to the newfound enthusiasm for religions from foreign cultures. The Fourth of July or Veterans' Day are simply days off with little celebration or appreciation of the ideals behind them. Even in Catholicism, there is no longer an emphasis on holy days or seasonal devotions. It is also true, however, that the concept of "letting go of attachment" in Eastern thought does not always impact on our rampant consumerism. In capitalist America, people who join an Eastern religion may still find themselves caught up in consumerism. This can even take the form of spiritual materialism that gathers spiritual experiences as if they were material goods. In the 1950s, people were proud of their new appliances whereas now they might boast of their support of Tibet or commitment to daily meditation.

Some people are realizing that no single religion or spiritual path is quite sufficient, and they design a synthesis of practices and beliefs. This makes sense since we need to draw from many sources to have an informed and full experience of anything in a world as complex as ours. The sad thing is that traditional churches have not joined in this movement toward integration, and the historical and spiritual wealth they can offer are less appealing to people who want to break out of parochialism.

At the same time, the Protestant work ethic still exerts a powerful influence on most Americans, 70 percent of whom still hold that God spiritually rewards those who are committed to working hard. It follows that those on welfare or in poverty are unsaved and have no one to blame for this but themselves. The move away from these old conservative theories by many liberals also accounts for the new interest in religions that break with the conservative and capitalist view. Mother Teresa was the great model of recapturing this in our time. (It must also be said that Christianity is not about siding with the poor against the rich but about addressing injustice.) These lines of Walt Whitman say something about America's religious destiny that is so often overlooked: "I believe the main purport of these States is to found a superb friendship, exalté, previously unknown, / because I perceive it waits, and has been always waiting, latent in all men."

In any healthy society, the speculating members at large are ahead of the conservators of the official constitution. Progress usually derives from just such tensions. The issue here is free speech so that change can occur and people can be acknowledged as adult, without fear of reprisals for speaking up. The issue here is public vs. private, not official magisterium vs. theological opinion. A healthy Church encourages dialogue so that teachings can be reformulated in accord with modern needs. When the official Church does this, it acts in accord with its mission of evangelization. "Difference is positive only within communion with the other: in respect of the other who is other and yet not alien to us," says Edward Schillebeeckx. Robert Bellah adds: "Disagreements are not so much a failure of consensus as they are evidence of the vigor of a debate over what the Church, and ultimately religion, is all about in our society."

Paul Tillich commented that anyone seeking meaning has religious faith. Bernard Lonergan adds that faith is possible without beliefs. Beliefs are intellectually formed affirmations consequent upon faith. Vatican II emphasized the community dimension of faith, that it happens fruitfully within a believing community. We are touched by the witness of others and so grow in faith, that is, we are moved by the lives of saints. It can also happen within ourselves and not in a community other than the broad human community. Adult faith is thus an engagement for action, something we do. It is following Christ's Sermon on the Mount. The saints are guides to the wise solutions and loving powers in ourselves. The statues we see in a church represent the potentials in us, realized in them. To light a candle to them is to proclaim the joyous and boundless possibilities of the life of faith and service.

People look at the institution, the antiquated laws, the repressive strictures and think that the Church is moribund. But the life of the Church is gauged by the vitality of its saints, the thousands of loving and wise people who live out the works of mercy every day of every year. Their charisms are impervious to institutional repressions or atavistic beliefs. The reliable presence of saints in the world is the evidence of the Spirit at work in time in communities of faith. No pope or rule can interfere with that evolutionary vigor. The Church is as alive today as it was in 100 A.D. There are just as many saints and martyrs, just as many teachers, just as many miracles, just as many loving commitments, just as many living incarnations of Jesus Christ. The institutional Church may take many decades for an aggiornamento. The saints take action in the now. They are not afraid to reinvent ritual and upgrade conscience to meet the challenges of the moment. What will it take for us to claim our rightful powers and our rightful responsibilities?

An example of a major projection of personal power and of the authority of the human conscience is the adulation of the papacy. The pope is the representation of the archetype of certitude. Our need for certitude is so extreme and our doubt in our own access to truth is so far gone that we still seem to require a leader who protects truth for us and proclaims it to us. The historical continuity of personal faith and of human cherishing of perennial truths does not seem to be enough for the scared ego. What then funds papal power is awe at the grandeur and display that flatter and safeguard the ego. That power is meant to be shared, not adored. The Self is the priest and pope that offer the ego as a sacrifice for redemption. We offer just such a Mass when we turn the other cheek rather than retaliate in kind, when we love rather than hate, when we live humbly rather than arrogantly. True dialogue between ego and its vast potentials in the Self shows up absolutism in any form as limiting and stunting. Only pluralism, the eternal enemy of the eternal city, works here.

The pope is among the last of the divine right monarchs in the Western world. A great gift to him and to all of us would be to restore him to his role as the servant of servants. Instead the veneration of the pope often assumes cultic proportions. Cults appeal to people who seek direction and inclusion. Cults thrive on idealization hunger. We attach ourselves either to gang leaders or to the Dalai Lama to feel a sense of meaning and belonging. The healthy alternative is admiration and cooperation. *Healthy adults do not need leaders; they need experts, advocates, assisting forces.*

When the pope is also a saint, however, he becomes the spiritual friend of the earth and of all humanity. The pope archetype carries the ego / Self axis by holding the burden of the opposites: great power and human lowliness. Thus it is a metaphor for our work in the world as servants of it and effective powers in its evolution. The world needs us as servants of the servants and as authoritative voices in our pointing to injustice. We are infallible when we speak in loving terms and see the meaning in history. The address "Your Holiness" is to the Higher Self in all of us.

Union with Christ... implies the radical sacrifice of egoism.
— PIERRE TEILHARD DE CHARDIN

FOUR

Challenges to Faith

Look deep into Nature,
and you will understand everything human.
— ALBERT EINSTEIN

Adult faith makes room within us to confront some fundamental facts about human existence. These are the givens of life that we may have believed it was the task of religion to assuage or even eradicate. But a mature faith does not reject reality; it addresses it. In high school geometry we began the problem-solving with givens: axiomatic facts not requiring proof. As part of our spiritual practice we attend to and accept the givens we keep noticing in life. The practice is how we till our souls in the garden of earthly givens. These three stand out: transitoriness, suffering, and aloneness.

Transitoriness

The seasons' difference.... These are counselors that feelingly
persuade me what I am. — As You Like It

The first given is that everything in life is transitory, changing, and not permanently satisfying. To the childish mind, this condition must be abrogated by fixation, addiction, and attempts to control. We keep attempting to force things to stay the same for us, to last for us. "Abide, thou art so fair," is how Faust said it.

We may deny that our interior geometry contains an inextricable bell-shaped curve: rising, cresting, falling. These are the three continually repeated phases of all our attractions and repulsions. To the adult, the given of transitoriness simply recalls that all things in life pass through stages and curves. We rise in fascination with a thing or place or person or idea. Then we hit a high point and crest. Finally, our fascination declines. When this happens, the healthy practice is to mourn the loss and move on to what comes next.

When a Roman emperor-elect walked in procession to receive his crown, he was interrupted three times by a slave who lit a quick-blazing flare in his face and said, "Sic transit gloria mundi." This same custom has carried over to the coronation of a pope. A priest, in unadorned black, steps between the pope and the pomp and says: "Holy Father, thus passes the glory of the world." Life lights that flare for us many times on the grandiose procession our ego makes through life. Nature balances our inflations with deflations again and again. We can say yes to this, or we can use people, places, things, or religion to stave off the inevitable truth of constant change. Adults get to be at home with the shape of concrete reality and land safely on it. Adolescents cannot see the inexorable impact of the conditions of existence on themselves because their egos are so inflated. They imagine they can conquer them all: never get old and wrinkled, never die. Maturity makes a fuller vision possible. That is the equivalent of the egoless view. In other words, letting go of ego makes it possible to be spiritual. It is a broader way of seeing.

St. Paul wrote: "When this earthly tent is folded up, there awaits us a tabernacle not made by hands." Christ said: "Heaven and earth will pass away but my words will not pass away." Religious statements speak to the terror of transitoriness. Every given is a terror to those who do not greet the cycles of life and death with equanimity. The promise that death is only a part of the human cycle and not an end to it is the joy of faith. But to be fully conscious, this promise and hope in the promise must coexist with the truth of transitoriness.

Mircea Eliade, in *Myth and Reality,* says that "initiation is a passing by way of symbolic death and resurrection from ignorance and immaturity to the spiritual age of an adult." If there is a way to blunt the ravages of transitory time, it is not literal (thing-oriented) but metaphorical and mythic. Initiation into the life of faith means dying to our petty claims to exemption from the conditions of existence in favor of rebirth to a new existence. This new existence is the one animated by the love that lets go of clinging and control. Love is the only and ultimate doorway beyond our mortal limits. To love unconditionally with a full yes to every condition of existence grants safe passage to new life. Such life is accessible in this immediate here and now. If we say that God is love here and now, then the God-life is here when love is here and it is in the now when love is happening now.

Once we say God is love, then the power of God is love, not force. In fact, power *is* love. In such a world, there is no room for punishment or retaliation. Justice finds a way to be merciful. To say that God is love is to affirm that love creates, sustains, redeems, and sanctifies the world. Love is the wholeness we were meant to express in our every gesture and choice. The result is an attitude of abiding thanks, a sense of being held and of having the power to hold the world in our hearts. Mother Teresa said it: "I am in Jesus' heart, and Jesus is in my heart." Any sense of something missing changes to a conviction that everything has been received.

"You ordered all things by measure, number, and weight," says the Book of Wisdom (11:21). The universe endlessly elaborates itself into the farthest reaches of space. *I am one such elaboration.* In this sense, there is no circumference to reality. Psyche is nature become conscious of itself. Absolute refers to the origin and life force of the ongoing evolutionary cycle. (The absolute is personified because our imagination is so enamored of images.) Since this cycle includes dissolution too, opposites alternate with one another and are united. Life is thus revealed in two phases: evolution and dissolution. The goal of spirituality is to welcome both. Then we are not devastated by the fact of dissolution but trust its phase-appropriateness. To come to the point of being able to say yes to its most terrifying costumes is true fortitude: "I am consoled that this is a phase that makes evolution possible and I can trust myself to live through. I am grateful to the assisting forces around and beyond me." There is always the option of finding solace in someone who will make it stop or fix it. The union of opposites seems to provide the most durable consolation.

We can also summon images of calm that reflect our potential to say yes to all the passing show of life and nature no matter how scary it becomes. Everything is a revelation of the Self ultimately since it is all just what it takes for evolution to proceed. To proceed with it, we ride the horse in the direction in which it is going. That ride is called yes to the givens of existence. It is the way we fulfill our human destiny to live gracefully among people and things. We are not here to live as long as we can but to live long enough to manifest the unconditional love, perennial wisdom, and healing power of our higher Self. The human ego asks "Why?" The universal psyche says "Yes!"

Impermanence also refers to the fact that life is unpredictable. We do not know our future. Present positive evidence gives no guarantee of a positive future. Present discouraging evidence does not necessarily presage disaster. The childish response to life's unpredictability is to seek out safe and reliable certitudes. "There will always be silver lining" is an immature wish meant to buy off the uncontrollable realities of life. It beguiles us away from the bluntness of truth. The adult response is simply to allow, to say yes unconditionally to what cannot be changed. This is the antidote to wishful thinking.

Adult faith happens in the paradoxical gap that opens in the human mind when confronted with (1) the apparent arbitrariness of nature and history *and* (2) a belief in an upholding and reliable providence. One and two seem irreconcilable, but the combining word "and" closes the gap. Simultaneously, we are held and we are not held; we are both in the grace of circumstance and at the mercy of circumstance. Nature is unpredictable as it moves toward an omega point of coherence. Faith accommodates a "both ... and" where logic sees only an "either ... or." Faith never expunges or simplifies our human story. It enriches it by the paradox of simultaneity, the union of opposites. The conditions of existence are sources of spontaneity, surprise, unexpected miracles, unpredictable turns of events, creative challenges and opportunities. *The conditions of existence are stimuli for the life force.* "Birth and death, arising and vanishing are themselves nirvana," says Dogen Zenji.

Providence is often invoked as a *deus ex machina* in the midst of crisis. Actually, providence means that in the face of suffering, cruelty, death, and injustice we have it in us to go on loving. This is how it "all works out for the best." It is not that external situations rectify themselves but that interior powers of love remain intact no matter what. Our capacity to love survives the pain and abuse we have experienced. That is the meaning of spiritual survival. It is also what is meant by providence as a power that upholds us.

Paul Tillich wrote in *The Shaking of the Foundations:* "Faith in divine providence is the faith that nothing can prevent us from fulfilling the ultimate meaning of our existence. Providence does not mean a divine planning by which everything is predetermined.... Providence means that there is a creative and saving possibility implied in every situation, which cannot be destroyed by any event. Providence means that the demonic and destructive forces within ourselves and our world can never have an unbreakable grasp upon us, and that the bond which connects us with the fulfilling love can never be disrupted."

The more the future opens before me like some dizzy abyss or dark tunnel, the more confident I may be — if I venture forward on the strength of your word — of losing myself and surrendering myself in you, of being assimilated by your body, Jesus.

— Pierre Teilhard de Chardin

Suffering

The second condition of existence is the universality of suffering. Every human life will include physical pain, emotional pain, and spiritual pain. A childish religious response to pain might be: I believe that evil-doers will be punished in this life or with eternal pain in hell, and/or I have a personal exemption: "It can't happen to me." Such beliefs are wishes that reality be fair, that someone or something mete out appropriate rewards and punishments.

Notice that "fairness" in this respect may mean a wish to punish those who cross us and thus be contrary to the Sermon on the Mount ("Love your enemies; do good to those who hurt you.") Jesus did not desire to punish but to transform. When we love one another, we never wish pain on those who are unjust. We wish their transformation. We let them be and we return love for evil. This is an adult faith response and happens more easily after we have felt our pain and grieved it. The adult accepts the unchangeable reality, no matter how "unfair," and pays attention to realities that can be changed. All this is done in a spirit of compassion. The wish to punish is puerile and itself evil. Rehabilitative compassion is the way of Christ and of enlightened masters.

It is understandable to think of Hitler in hell. Is it possible to think of him in an everlasting monastery with an abbot who equips his soul to see the suffering he caused and shows him how to repent so that by the end of time he might be ready to ask forgiveness from everyone he hurt? Hell and monastery are both metaphors, so why not the latter rather than the former? Is it not more advantageous to have an abbot instead of a devil in my consciousness? It makes for more love in my own hurt and at times hurtful heart.

To insist that suffering not be a part of life in any way is to say no to a given of existence. That no is the cause of more suffering. Fidelity to ourselves requires that we engage with our own inner struggles long enough to gain their blessing, like Jacob wrestling the angel. We can accept and endure pain and wait for its meaning to reveal itself to us — or not. We can also console ourselves in the midst of it with a belief in its ultimate meaning or in the silver lining within it. "Meaning makes things endurable, perhaps everything," wrote Jung. Is the meaning we find based on imagination or on reality? That is the ultimate question for adults. There is indeed a positive dimension to everything when the teaching can be found in it and we have not lost our ability to receive it.

St. Teresa of Avila said: "When we accept what happens to us and make the best of it, we are praising God." Pain accepted and worked with fosters a spiritual photosynthesis. "We are transformed by what we accept. We transform what we have accepted by understanding it," says Govinda. "Accept" in this context does not mean resignation to pain but an entrance into it, a penetration of it, and a release from it. Penetration involves finding a kernel of value in it. What makes life meaningful is the evolution of consciousness through the events that happen to us, painful and otherwise. What makes it exciting is our commitment to that conscious yes everywhere and in everything. Suffering is a necessary part of the evolution of consciousness. In fact, all the conditions of existence are the specific *requisites* for becoming people of character, depth, and compassion. The suffering servant is the archetype of how consciousness can redeem pain.

Pain toughens us. An incoherent, fragile, or unstable person could not live out the hero path. It takes a strong ego but not a retaliatory, bloated, or controlling one. Pain provides an impetus toward individuation and a doorway to higher consciousness. This is a spiritual consciousness since it defies ego explanations. A higher power has to be acknowledged and accessed, that is, a higher consciousness, God. The pain that happens to us is pedagogy. It teaches us how to let go of fear and desire, to find our deepest needs, values, and wishes, and to fulfill our destiny. Pain is the price of these opportunities for evolution.

If the suffering we undergo becomes conscious to us in this way, it redeems itself. In fact, redemption in the Christian myth is precisely this: Christ chose to be placed at the mercy of evil *as a spiritual practice* and thereby redeemed the evil done to him. Suffering then is a practice rather than an affliction that is imposed on a victim or a penalty imposed on a culprit. Keats wrote in a letter: "How then are souls to be made? How then are these sparks which are God to have identity given them — so as ever to possess a bliss peculiar to each one's individual existence? How but by the medium of a world like this? . . . Do you not see how necessary a world of pain and troubles is to school an intelligence and make it a Soul? A place where the heart must feel and suffer in a thousand diverse ways!"

Pain has worked for us when it leads to a greater consciousness of our psycho-spiritual identity, a respect for the givens of existence rather than expecting indulgence in the face of them. This means less entitlement to special treatment, more compassion, more humor, more effective relationships, and a sense of being part of a whole, of living in communal context. In the *Gospel of Thomas,* people dance around Christ, who is standing cheerfully in the center.

An evolutionary function of suffering is to experience it for the whole of humankind. We suffer something and thereby know how to help others who suffer it too. Experience does more than teach us; it equips us to become healers. We are all interrelated, so our suffering not only deepens us but enables us to understand and assist others when their pain is similar to our own. Pain is a path to compassion, one taken by all the saints. Saints are those who put their own conviction to live in love above selfish gain or even survival.

Wounds are identification marks, as St. Thomas learned. In the image of his wounded and light-emitting heart, Jesus says: "This is what I am." Jesus found his full identity through his wounds. Our scars present our identity even physically inasmuch as everyone has a different set of them in different places, forming a unique design on the body. The questions are: How is this pain connected to the totality of our lives? How does this crisis reveal us to ourselves? What is the loving intent in the universe that makes this a gift?

The *I Ching* says: "It is only when we have the courage to accept things as they are, without any sort of self-deception or illusion, that a light will develop out of events, by which the path to success may be recognized." Development happens by affirming responses from our parents and friends throughout life. Inner character develops the same way, through our affirming responses to our predicaments. In fact, the difference between suffering that hinders growth or helps it happen is that neurotic suffering resists the conditions of existence while authentic suffering deals with them.

Resurrection is the archetype of hope, a way of acknowledging that suffering and death are not final. This animates us in ways that lead to individuation. Pentecost — the animation of the disciples by the Holy Spirit — directly results from the Resurrection. It is all one ongoing and coherent initiation. Pain is the characteristic of any initiatory process. Death and the cross are conditions of transformation, not just conditions of existence. That is the good news of redemption. Ovid in his *Fasti VI* stated it too: "There is a god in us who, stirring, kindles us."

Finding serenity and resting in its sequestered sanctuary is not the adult program in the face of pain. Such tranquillity can itself become an object of attachment or a distraction from the path. The reality is beyond peace and conflict in a realm that transcends and allows them. The real refuge of faith is reality. To sit or walk in mindfulness is to contact it.

When there is a disaster in a plane, pilots are trained to take an inventory of what they have going for them rather than to fixate on what has gone wrong. Chaos is the prime matter for a creative response and solution. At the same time, Jung reminds us: "Sometimes the divine asks too much of us." Sometimes nothing can be done and we confront "the things that cannot be changed." Hanging on the cross in full consciousness of so many contradictions was Jesus' spiritual practice: "He refused to drink." This is difficult for those taught to do something about anything uncomfortable. Yet a vision of divine meaning happens only after suffering has been endured. Job found this out: "*Now* my eye has seen thee."

The mention of Job leads to the conundrum "Why do the innocent suffer?" This question presupposes that the guilty *should* suffer and the innocent *should* be happy. This is juvenile wish, not reality. To an adult, indiscriminate pain is not taken personally. It is a given of probability. Suffering is not meant as punishment for evil any more than joy is meant as a reward for goodness. Nothing interrupts our history to make sure everything follows such a plan. Suffering happens even in the context of the firmest connection to the divine: "I and the Father are one," were the words of one cruelly and unjustly betrayed and crucified.

The suffering referred to here is an evil, but it is an unplanned evil. It differs from the evil of an injustice that is maliciously planned, chosen, and implemented. Suffering is an evil in accord with nature's laws. Deliberate malice is an evil that is human-made and deliberately inflicted. The suffering of life is to be expected and handled with care by us and with caring for others. Deliberate evil is to be confronted and fought, never accepted passively or apathetically.

Why does God not intervene in human injustice? Why did God not halt the Holocaust or stop a rape or murder? These are questions that expect God to be coercive. It is not the nature of the Self to interrupt human freedom. It impels; it does not compel. Evolution shows the noncoercive and nonsudden style of creation. Everything real takes time to develop and includes a dark chapter. A life opens to cycles and seasons. A full conception of the divine will include the elements of the Hindu trinity: creation, destruction, and preservation. All three are permitted and all three have there own timing. To omit the dark side is to impoverish divine wholeness and to contradict the evidence of nature. Adult hope is not based on divine interventions but on the third force: preservation. Life goes on and suffering is redeemed. The promise of faith is not that bad things will not happen to good people but that goodness will survive and that good people can become better through it all.

The given of suffering in life includes a given of malice and evil.

This is what Jung referred to as the shadow side of ourselves and of society. War, the Holocaust, atomic weapons, international terrorism, represent the societal given of evil. A personal given is our penchant to be dishonest, hurtful, violent, or malicious. We are the perpetrators of evil. We are the victims of evil not of our own making. Perhaps this is the metaphorical meaning of "original sin."

The challenge of adult faith is to believe in design despite display. The display is what occurs in our story. The design is the transcendent reality that underlies all of history, synchronously and randomly challenging our capacity to grow through pain. Faith accepts the fact of the givens and the fact that miracles occasionally break through to defy the givens on our behalf. Having faith means the capacity to love which endures no matter what the impact of the events.

Asceticism and the choice for pain is not the path that helps us grow. Many people in history became saints under the most life-denying and self-negating conditions. But that happened not because of those conditions but in spite of them. Hurt, hate, and betrayal — though never to be sought — figure in the making of the hero. Joseph could not sell himself into slavery; he had to be betrayed into it by his brothers. Jonah could not jump overboard to meet the whale; he had to be thrown by the ship's crew. Jesus did not turn himself over to the Sanhedrin; he was betrayed to them by Judas. Dorothy could get from the Kansas of status quo to the Oz of wonder only by being thrown there by a tornado. In every instance, the heroes progress toward their destiny because of the effect of an evil. Perhaps many who hurt or disappointed us "threw" us out of our comfortable delusions and helped us find our personal character, strength, and truth.

Emerson says in his *Essay on Experience:* "We should not postpone and refer and wish, but do broad justice where we are, by whomsoever we deal with, accepting our actual companions and circumstances, however humble or odious, as the mystic officials to whom the universe has delegated its whole pleasure for us." Synchronicity, meaningful co-incidence, happens through a series of similar events. A man loses his job, finds out his wife is having an affair, totals his car, and learns he has cancer of the prostate in the course of a year. These events are certainly the ingredients for despair when all we have is our egos. But perhaps there is a loving intent in all that occurs. What if all these things have happened for a purpose?

The purposes of the higher Self *are* the Self: unconditional love, contact with our inner wisdom, and healing balance in our lives. Perhaps all that happens to us happens so that we can finally let go of our controlling or driven ego and learn to love more. Perhaps crises are meant to give us a push away from a passive or stultifying routine. Perhaps they instill a sense of vulnerability and the need for trust in powers beyond ourselves.

Dreams and images that arise at these straitening and terrifying times often reveal the meanings in the crises. The loving intent in what has happened to us is also revealed by *what the events made us do.* For instance, we have to ask for help now and were too self-sufficient to do that before. We have become more tender or compassionate, traits that may have been out of character for us before all this happened.

Synchronous events in life are not just coincidences and bad breaks; they are breakthroughs of the spiritual into our too time-encapsulated lives. Here are some questions that may help us find the depth and meaning of our life story: "What is the question for which this provides the answer?" "How can this help me love more?" "How is this helping me *be* more?"

> *The Fall...is an event which blasted man's opportunity to de-*
> *velop — without suffering, violence, despair, and death, though*
> *not...without tension and trial — the rich resources and large*
> *potentialities for the human spirit.*
>
> — Barbara Keifer Lewalski,
> "Innocence and Experience in Milton's Eden"

Aloneness

Almost any pain can be endured when a companion appears and stays with us as we go through it. In the Christian myth, God not only sent; he came. *Can we stay with ourselves that way?* At the same time, the third given of life is aloneness. Each of us lives our lives as a single person; each is born and dies alone. For those of us who were not born as Siamese twins, our life is unique to us and a solo experience.

The childish response is to fill ourselves with external events, people, and dramas. The adult approach is to appreciate the solitude while still reaching out to others and enjoying their company. An adult accepts periods of aloneness as important to the process of growth. This is an archetypally feminine feature of the hero's work. Jack was hidden in the cupboard (womb) by the giant's wife before his daring battle. Bellerophon kept vigil in the temple of Athena before fighting the Chimera. His reward for staying was a magic bridle to tame the Pegasus, given to him by the goddess. In both metaphors, female assistance came to the hero after his willingness to be alone and contained. The archetypal and alchemical motif of containment is a crucial piece on the board of transformation. Christ in the womb of Mary is the Christian example of this same period of gestation within the female container before the Epiphany occurs. Containment-in-preparation is a spiritual way of reckoning periods of aloneness on our journey.

Again and again in scripture, there are phrases that speak to our aloneness: "I will fear no evil for thou are with me"; "Stay with us Lord, for the evening comes"; "Behold I am with you all days." There is in the psyche a sense of a protecting presence that ends or cuts through isolation. But sometimes the sense of presence disappears in the face of a terrifying existential absence. Christ felt this on Calvary. "Why hast thou forsaken me?" He shared in our greatest terror: to be abandoned, utterly alone. This was the very thing the scriptures seem to have promised would never happen. But Jesus is the archetype of the redeeming power of accepting the given of aloneness. His share in human forsakenness shows it to be bearable, legitimate, temporary, and redemptive.

Every great mystic felt this aloneness, though each was a person of faith. So *faith does not exempt us from this or any given of human existence*. Not one given will be repealed, abolished, or annulled just for us. We have no entitlement to special treatment. There are no disclaimers in adulthood. The leap of faith is from the childish belief that religion offers a reliable consoling end to aloneness to the mature belief that aloneness coexists with faith. Childhood's "either...or" continually gives way to "both...and."

In fact, taking refuge in God does not mean finding a refuge from the conditions of existence but becoming a refugee in the midst of them, like our forebear, Jesus. Often we find no answer in the face of life's unfairly distributed tortures. The predicament of finding no answer *is* the void. Despair is the void. It has no dimension, and that is what is so terrifying about its isolation.

Aloneness can feel like a deep vacancy within us. Then it scares us with a sense of personal emptiness and the absence of any support. Aloneness can also feel like a deep *spaciousness* within us, one that opens onto a vast, explorable horizon. Then it is positive and gladdens us with a sense of presence. A consequent sense of an accompanying presence is, in effect, the other side of our joy in our own presence. The negative aloneness leads to a sense of loneliness and worthlessness, which we attempt to erase with attachments and addictions. This is our neurotic ego holding on to something that can fix us. The positive aloneness leads to solitude and inner worth, which make us receptive to what next may bloom. This is our healthy ego not holding on but feeling held. The irony is that we feel held precisely when we no longer hold on. "If I should go to the farthest ends of the earth, even there your hand is holding me" (Ps. 139).

Neurotic aloneness with its frantic hunger for distractions is a hole in us. The functional aloneness with its abundance to give is the whole in us. When I ask myself "Who am I?" how quickly I answer with a list of characteristics that delineate my roles and choices in life. But this list tells me exactly who I am not. Roles and choices are meant to satisfy my desire to fill myself from the outside and find approval in the bargain.

Aloneness is the path to who we are: nothing but space for what is here and now and what may be. Giving up the illusion that others make us whole, we gain a sense of wholeness in our solitude. We notice both our spaces and our boundaries. We automatically know how to take care of ourselves. This combination of receptiveness: "an unconditional Yes to that which is," as Jung says, and self-nurturance in the midst of what is, turns out to be the most adult identity card we carry.

> *What is demanded of man is not to endure the meaninglessness of life, but rather to bear his incapacity to grasp its unconditional meaningfulness in rational terms.* — VIKTOR FRANKL

Standing Alone at the Edge of the Void

> *When he opened the seventh seal, there was silence in heaven.*
> — REVELATION 8:1

The Void is the terrifying sense of irremediable desolation that occurs for all of us from time to time in life. Sometimes it is triggered by a crisis or loss. Sometimes it happens for no apparent reason. It can vanish as mysteriously as it arrives. The Void confronts us with a stubborn silence beyond our ability to escape or interrupt it. This dark night of encircling gloom is felt only as emptiness, vacancy, a wilderness with no oasis. No amount of self-esteem can override or evade it. It is a condition beyond conditions.

The terror in the Void is the sense of abandonment by every spiritual support. If prayer works, it is not the Void. If activities work, it is not the Void. If anything works, it is not the Void. The terror in this spiritual panic attack is that nothing works to save us from the vacuum into which we have been thrown. The experience of the Void means no foothold, no handle on things, no end in sight, no light at the end of the tunnel. It is not quite adequately described as aloneness, loneliness, emptiness, forsakenness, abandonment, desperation, isolation, or even despair. It is all of these at once!

The Void is the shadow of the mind. It is the hidden, unreliable side of our functional ego. To say that "nothing works" in the Void means that the mind, no matter how intelligent or functional, goes bankrupt when the chips are truly down. Its half measures avail nothing in the face of the true terror. The Void is the Sherlock Holmes who exposes the ego as the Great Pretender.

In the Void, we cannot defend ourselves as we always have. What a paralyzing experience for the ego, with its all its clever ruses, its trusty bag of tricks, its stratagems to maintain control, its belief it is entitled not to have things like this happen! Now it is ambushed by a seditious and invisible militia. The ego is confronting its actual condition in the adult world: it has no real ground on which to stand securely. It is No-Thing. This is, paradoxically, the true meaning both of psychological panic and of spiritual awakening to egolessness. The panic about the Void dramatizes the inadequacy of ego and the spiritual destiny of ego to go beyond its power games and face its utter fragility. Such egolessness is a liberation into the larger truth about who we are.

From earliest life, the prospect of being dropped may have filled us with terror. This is just such a drop from invisible arms. To go into such a free-fall space feels like annihilation — becoming nothing. In the direct encounter with remedyless and solutionless aloneness, we realize that every clever charm, every gesture, every source of ready consolation has fallen flat. We are being given a direct, unblurred vision of our ultimate condition with a simultaneous crash of all the means we ever employed to avoid it. Our usual condition is to find that things work, that the world we built for ourselves houses us well. Now we find that there is another side: darker, more frightening, merciless, totally adamant against seduction or cajoling. It allows no loopholes. It is not fooled by our coquettishness.

The habits, bulwarks, dramas, relationships, addictions, and people that we gathered around us helped us stave off this ultimate moment of truth. They joined us in the game of avoidance of the Void, avoidance of full surrender of ego. But all that is really collapsing here is the illusion of security. *Only illusion can collapse.* Our shell, our armor is being dismantled. Our true inner Self remains. In the terror of this moment, such a realization may not be a comfort. Our main fear may be *not* being able to die then and there!

Now what? When we simply pay attention to the Void, the inner stagnation may awaken and begin to live in a new way. To face the naked truth about ourselves nakedly is all we can or need to do. The Void is a mirror of the "space" that is ourselves. Meister Eckhart says: "Everything is *meant* to be lost that the soul may stand in unhampered nothingness." The Void is actually a special grace that takes us beyond the mind and its tricks. We can now confront our condition of aloneness instead of using so many consolations and distractions to protect ourselves from it.

We experience the Void as especially scary because we have been refusing to face the fact of our aloneness and of the inadequacy of our every defense. This is how we betrayed the fearlessness that was always living within us. Our armoring, our running, our running for help, every thought, every plan, every hope we ever cherished: all were ways of forestalling our inevitable encounter with this inner silence. The Void is the emptiness we always assumed we had to fill but actually only had to face. "Was every choice I made, every activity I chose, a way of eluding this trickster that wanted to call me by name?"

The Void is ultimately mind. It is not a real entity. It is a mirror of our own nonsolidity. Void means void of boundaries, as is the true Self. When we sit it out, the Void surrounds us but does not extinguish us. We simply stay as "the evening comes." We sit still and allow every feeling to pass through us and go to ground as lightning flashes through a rod. We feel no ground but let our feelings go to ground.

"Lost to myself, I stayed," says St. John of the Cross. We get through the Void (not around or past it) by sitting through its severest threats. The practice of mindfulness is the path through the Void. We simply stay in suspense. We just hang there, as Jesus did on the cross. We lie there, as he did in the tomb. We simply sit, as Buddha did under the tree. We lie, as Osiris did in his temple at Philae, still giving life while supine. He is shown lying in the stillness of death, yet in just that way he is the source of light at the end of death's dark corridor. Such a combination of opposites can only be the Self, the All in all of us: "The genuine word of eternity is spoken only in eternity, where man is a desert and alien both to himself and multiplicity," writes Meister Eckhart.

If nothing works and we still survive, we have learned that there is nothing to fear ever again. "I survived without support" means "I have no need of my usual supports." We discover the surprising paradox: our challenge is *not* to fill ourselves. Being a hollow bamboo does the most to help us grow into spiritual adulthood. We embrace total disillusionment and are thereby free from despair. Despair means no hope to hold on to. When we throw away the hope of exemption from the conditions of human existence and notice that we still survive, we are liberated from dependency on hope and liability to despair. We walk the path *between* these extremes. Then the silence in heaven becomes what a Hermetic hymn declares: "The angels sing in silence."

When we stay with our life processes, a new softness happens in our hearts. As one author says: "The mind creates the abyss; the heart crosses it." We become more accessible to the truths of existence, more open to the unprotected and unsupported moments in our lives. The Void is, after all, only unconditional being. It is our experience of existence without the tassels and booties we put on it so we will never hear its thud. This unconditional being is actually our higher Self. It is what we are after all the doing, acting, and defending have been removed. Our "unique characteristics" are really a set of standard — even fixated — habits and poses that make life more comfortable for us. At base we are open, that is, not yet filled with meanings, concepts, postures, rigid armoring. Void means void of all that. What frightens us is seeing ourselves without our psychological trimmings. All we have been avoiding is our own identity. The mind has gazed into a mirror of itself. It has seen the simulacrum of its empty face, the pure space that is its actual identity: *The Void is I.*

Actually, the experience of the Void is a summons, a call to the adventure of poise beyond pose, of Self beyond ego, of love beyond fear. The Void is a farther reach of our own potential, now beckoning to us to actualize it. The sense of inner emptiness is the experience of ourselves as the alchemical vessel of transformation. Thomas Merton said that "a deep existential anxiety crisis precedes the final integration of the Self." The Void is the threshold to rebirth beyond fear. This is because forsakenness is a necessary ingredient of spiritual maturity. Without it, we might never have learned to look within. We would have trusted only external sources, as children trust parents. Without forsakenness, we would have looked only outside for nurturance. We would have maintained the neediness of childhood, never freeing up the plenipotentiary powers of adulthood.

When we shake the pillars that hold up our temple of defenses, we join in the demolition of our frightened childish belief system. In the rubble, we see every false premise, every shred and patch that held our life together, every superstition, every wish for safety from the full brunt of the human story. This is the edifice that collapses, not the fortress of true supports and nurturance but the stockade of imprisoning delusions. We never had anything to lose but our chains.

James Hillman says: "Moments of dissolution are not mere collapses; they release a sense of personal human value from the encrustations of habit." Dissolution is a stage in the alchemical process of releasing the fearless, that is, unconditional, Self — the authentic identity we have been avoiding all along. The Void thus prompts a giant leap into finding out who we really are: *We are love in the habit of fear.* Now we see why we believed we had to maintain control: to avoid an encounter with the inner emptiness that fear disguised. To drop control and face our fear is to open the inner spaciousness that love designed.

"When this ultimate crisis comes, when there is no way out, that is the very moment when we explode from within and the totally other emerges. . . . It is the sudden surfacing of a strength, a security of unknown origin, welling up from beyond reason, rational expectation, or hope." In the last words of this statement, Emil Durkheim defines grace. To find ourselves still standing after every munification has fallen means that we are supported by more than what we believed were our supports. This is the Epiphany, the appearance of the divine, the numinous moment when all that can remain is the ruthless faith that goes on believing, not because life has turned out well but because life has renewed itself once again.

We try so hard to avoid ever having to face the Void. Yet, to contain and relax into our own emptiness makes room for a deeply compassionate love to emerge. Vacancy becomes spaciousness, and we open ourselves to all who suffer as we do. This is how aloneness plays a key role in the release of unconditional love. It may seem that the Void and all the givens of existence are negative or even punitive. Actually, they are the necessary ingredients of human evolution and of true spiritual maturity. This poem of St. John of the Cross summarizes and declares it all in such a consoling way:

> *I entered I knew not where,*
> *And there I stood not knowing:*
> *Nothing left to know.*
> *I had entered the house of unknowing*
> *And knew not where I was.*
> *What great things I heard*
> *I cannot tell;*
> *I was there as one who did not know:*
> *Nothing left to know.*
>
> *Of peace and devotion*
> *My experience was perfect,*
> *My solitude profound.*

So secret was it
Even I could only stammer.
I had nothing left to know.

I stood beside myself in ecstasy enraptured;
My senses vanished, every one.
I had the gift of understanding,
Yet was I understanding nothing:
Nothing left to know.

The higher my achievement,
The less was left of me.
All that I had known
Was worth nothing now.
This newborn wisdom grew
Till I knew nothing at all
And had nothing left to know.

The higher I ascended,
The less I comprehended.
O dark fog that gives the night a glow.
To understand is not to comprehend
When there is nothing left to know.

This knowing that knows nothing
Has such power
That reason can't defeat it,
Or ever penetrate the depth of heart
That understands the nothing left to know.
What sovereign wisdom this is,
Beyond what science can ever attain!
He who dares to go beyond the mind
To the Knowing-Unknowing,
Always will come back alive,
But with nothing left to know.

Only listen and this wisdom
Reveals itself: a voice from heaven!
It was divine compassion all along
That left me naught to know.

(Author's translation)

Religion and the Givens

Adult faith is grounded in total allegiance to human conditions, in serene acknowledgment of the merciless laws of nature and the often more merciless choices of human beings, and in capacities for restoration and redemption. In other words, adult faith is grounded in our commitment to create lovingly alternative responses to every given and condition, and our faith is grounded in the hope that this alternative history of life will indeed triumph in the end. Until that time we will continue to pray for the grace to remain faithful despite apparent failure, recognizing that while this way of life leads sometimes to scorn, derision, imprisonment, and the cross, it is the only alternative to the lock-step march of dominant history toward war and death.

—*Catholic Agitator*, Spring 1991

Mature religion has two contributions to make: it gives counsel about facing the conditions of existence and points to the meaning in them. We may have believed that religion was supposed to reverse or soften the blows of the conditions of life. When we notice it does not work that way, we may "lose our faith." "If there were a God, he would not have permitted the Holocaust." In adult faith, we accept the noninterference of the divine in human choice. We accept that nothing immunizes us to the nature of things. "These are the tears of things," as Virgil said, landing on reality.

We are part of nature, and her conditions are ours. Nature accepts and repairs the catastrophes of weather, earth, and sea. Our interior realm of consciousness is the equivalent of space in the external world. Equilibrium in nature is the equivalent of equanimity in us. Our challenge is to accept and repair or, if repair is impossible, to accept and move on. The conditions of nature, no matter how distressing, are part of the necessary evolutionary cycle. The givens of our lives, no matter how disturbing, are the building blocks of our character and growth. Hamlet speaks admiringly of Horatio: "A man that fortune's buffets and rewards hast ta'en with equal thanks."

An adult with faith embraces the givens of existence not as heinous flaws in the universe but as essential facts. We are not victimized by these conditions. They make our life rich and our struggle challenging. The healthy adult honors and acknowledges life's givens with both grief and joy. We grieve the loss inherent in each and rejoice in the manifold variety and surprise of human living. We become really present on earth. Real presence means unconditional presence. The question is not whether God is present but whether we are willing to be.

To ask for a God who repeals the conditions of existence for us is to ask for a rescuer, not a higher power. It is to seek exception to what is. But if *what is* is *God's will,* where is faith in seeking such an exception? Religion negates life when it provides an escape from the givens, a "but" instead of an "and" to each of them. "I am alone but not really" changes to "I am truly alone and I trust in a support beyond myself that I may not always feel."

Faith is real when it includes every given with no entitlement to a repeal and pushes us out to take our chances on involvement with a humanity that grants no guarantees. Christ is the perfect example of this: "For he did not deem equality with God something to be clung to, but became human even to dying on the cross" (Phil. 2:6–8).

What does an adult need spiritually? The child seeks a safe haven from the full gamut of human experience. The adult finds a new center of gravity and a new form of sustenance. "I am the living bread that has come down from the heaven," Christ announced. The one who touched down on earth to touch and be touched in every human way is the model of personal nurturance. He hovered over every condition of existence and reverently whispered: "This is my body." And he said this as the Bridegroom of humanity.

Faith means accepting every condition of human existence, as Christ did. All eventualities become authorized and legitimate. "Yes, it can all happen to me. I am no exception. I accept the best of times and the worst of times, a time to live and a time to die and at the same time, I do — and sometimes fail to do — everything humanly possible to end suffering."

Eastern and Western monasticism gave us a tool for embracing the conditions of existence. Mindful attention to them leads to awakening. This form of prayer happens when we sit meditatively aware of our breathing no longer under the influence of our thoughts and judgments. We let go of the need to attach ourselves to our story or its outcome. We stay with our breath rather than be suffocated by fear, clinging, shame, control, or the need to change or fix things. Letting go of ego is the result of just such continual witnessing of impermanence.

Serenity in any circumstance may be a gift or a result (but not the purpose) of a meditation practice. Mindfulness meditation alone cannot provide that. Meditation can reveal our unconscious fears and wishes and free us from them. This is how it assists and supplements our psychological work. Meditation evokes unconscious material into consciousness. That awareness then loosens the hold that same material had on us. This is how it is liberating. It seems that therapy and religious practices are necessary adjuncts to meditation and vice versa. We go to therapy because religion does not have all the answers. We are religious because therapy is likewise inadequate.

Mindfulness meditation, befriending our shadow (dark) side, therapy, and religious rituals coordinate a response to pain that frees us from the ego layers and reveals the pearl in the oyster. Milton in Book VII of *Paradise Lost* refers to this as the "orient light exhaling first from darkness." Pain itself is never so bad as the layers of self-blame, shame, and fear, that we add to it. Our imagined layers of interpretations and translations, mostly shame-based or fear-based, make pain more difficult than it might be in itself. The problem is the gap between what is and how we see it, need it to be, or regret it having been. The ego layers also hide the kernel of value in it, and so we lose both coming and going.

In mindful awareness, the givens are revealed not as obstacles but as vehicles. A personal experience of loss, for instance, is precisely the encounter with transitoriness that becomes the first stop toward enlightenment. Once we appreciate that impermanence is the only reliable reality, we recognize the conditions of existence as Christ consciousness, Buddha mind. Then the experience of transitoriness *is* the realization of our higher Self.

In the face of life's givens, we feel not dismay but creative tension between opposites: impermanence and the endless cycles of death and resurrection. The death can be desolation, but it becomes consolation when new life appears from its ashes. The image of conscious death is that of a ripe apple falling into a mother's lap. We are the apples, and earth is our body's mother as the Great Mother of all the living and dying is our heavenly one.

Life and death, growth and decay, activity and rest are not irreconciliably opposing forces but interconnecting and interacting ingredients of the human story. Mindfulness meditation is a direct gaze at the pure and unadorned reality of life with its givens of change and enduring. Nature is both transient *and* cyclical. This means that we can despair and feel hope. We can see desolation and believe in restoration. This is how mindfulness contributes to faith. There is a direct proportion between commitment to meditation and growth in compassion. This is how it contributes to love.

There are two thrusts in the spiritual journey: the desire to escape from mortality while honoring and benefiting from it and the desire to contact immortality within and beyond ourselves. "Union with God" is the theological term for wholeness, the combining of mortal and immortal in oneself and in the nature of things. Since the divine life of the psyche-universe works in unfathomable and alogical ways, union with God turns out to be an assent to those natural ways, that is, to the conditions of existence. These include creation and destruction, change, impermanence, suffering. An unconditional yes to these givens is a powerful form of reverence. Consent to the orderly plan is oneness with *what is,* another way of saying yes to the "divine will." To say yes to what is makes us one with God: we become the immovable ground and expanding space beneath the conditions and contingencies of existence. Our yes is our transportation to transcendence when it means not just accepting the conditions of existence but being thankful for them and cooperating with them. This is how "all things work together unto good."

Perhaps this chapter ends best with a question: What if we were meant to grow as much from joy as we do from pain, as much from serenity as we do from crisis, as much from love as we do from loss?

Redemption is a separation and deliverance from an earlier con-dition of darkness and unconsciousness, and leads to a condition of illumination and victory over everything "given."

                                                — CARL JUNG

FIVE

Inner Truth, Religious Truth

God spoke in diverse ways.
—Hebrews 1:1

It is the role of religious symbols to give a meaning to life....
Modern people do not understand how much their rationalism
(which has destroyed their capacity to respond to the numinous)
...puts them at the mercy of the psychic underworld.
— CARL JUNG

Literal vs. Metaphorical

A metaphor is a recognition that an external reality has an inner life in us. A living metaphor is ontological, related to being, not allegorical, related to speech. A true metaphor moves from content (an image or story) to context (a personal connection to one's own story). An image strikes us and excavates a truth from deep in our psyche. It then loops back to the original content, and that becomes more meaningful since it is now felt in a personal or even transpersonal way. This is how an archetypal image begins to feel numinous. It depicts and recruits spiritual forces.

Metaphors communicate with consciousness and unconscious at once. While the conscious mind listens to the story, the unconscious mind wakens to new awarenesses. Metaphor becomes healing when it reframes our behavior or gives us a new way of appreciating the landscapes of our journey. A metaphor takes us on a journey from explication to implication. We gaze at a dove and become profoundly aware that its flight implies a capacity in us to soar to spiritual heights. Then the dove becomes a sacred symbol of a Holy Spirit, the divine capacity for enlightenment.

A child sees the divine-human archetypes corporeally as witches and demons and easily believes in the literal truth of them. Most of us were presented with a literal picture of religious truth. We imagined that all the events in Christ's life actually happened in exactly the ways the Bible describes. New scholarship in this century has shown us that the Bible is a faith document and not a news report. The Bible uses metaphor to tell about an experience of faith. It was never intended to provide a linear record of historical events in the Western style.

Literalism is a defense against the depth reality of religious experience. It reduces the mystery of a faith experience to a story. Adults see through stories. "Losing our faith" may mean simply losing our literalism. Something remains for those who appreciate and honor the depth of the psyche. It is the ground of being that lives through and beyond story. In fact, the story of our own life contains the mysterious revelation that we are more than we seem. Dogen Zenji, the thirteenth-century Buddhist master and poet, says: "*This* birth and death is the life of Buddha." Our life story is the story of the divine life. *The divine is that which we contact in the moment in which we touch the depth of our being, life, and purpose.*

All spiritual and religious truths are mysteries. Literal descriptions do not have the capacity to describe or even approximate the infinite. For that the imagination is required. Only in figurative language, poetry, and metaphor can the deepest human and divine realities be presented. Once we appreciate the metaphors in all the stories we remember, we expand our faith in the divine life. We see it in a more expansive and living way. For example, after the Resurrection, Jesus appears to the disciples eating honey and fish (Luke 24). This scene is a metaphor for aliveness without having to be a proof that Jesus is alive in a bodily way. So much of our religious education had to do with proving the literal truth of our beliefs. These were attempts to make ego-sense of something that is ineffable. The emphasis on proving is an attempt not to have to have faith.

The deepest reality uses symbols and images that embody it more adequately than intellectual description. The challenge of faith is to trust that there is something in us that transcends our mind and its ways of knowing. Faith relies on the depth perception in the Self: intuition, vision, imagination, assent to realities that defy explanation or even logical comprehension. These are the vehicles of revelation. The challenge of faith is to see with the eyes of the Self. We then recognize that these eyes are both the divine center and the human ground of reality.

Religion, like psychology, can produce only models of a reality the infinite reaches of which cannot be adequately measured. To codify it or define it as permanently and finally expressed is to diminish the mystery. A living mythologem cannot be expressed once and for all or once completely. It is a too-many-splendored thing. We think of revelation as located in books, thus limiting the limitless. It comes to us in every form of human communication, including nature and life events, and is directed to us in a *personal* way. It is not a book to read but a limitlessly expanding cyberspace of human consciousness.

Archetypes are evolving, like revelation and consciousness. We limit the evolutionary nature of human development when we imagine that revelation is closed. It is alive in every way that we are. It walks to us on every avenue of understanding of anything human, divine, or natural. The source of this knowledge emerges from within our consciousness, not from somewhere else. Tablets from Sinai contain the words of an inner Sinai. Revelation happens in continuity and contact with our interior life. *The word of God is inner wisdom that has found its way into external signs and messages.* Revelation is an encounter with the inner images that arise from the unconscious and reflect higher consciousness, that is, a higher power. The fact that the human psyche is the mediator of the divine does not make it unreal any more than two hands clasping in the dark make one of them unreal. In fact, attachment to orthodoxy can prevent access to a unique discovery of divine life in the personal psyche.

Enduring religious doctrines contain a powerful and archetypal kernel of truth. They reveal the larger life of the psyche and how it evolves toward individuation and enlightenment. If it becomes tied to one time or culture, it becomes fear-based and loses its lively energy. That is how we lose out on the wonderful riches in it. There are multiple and illimitable theophanies in accord with the multiple capacities and multiple avenues of accessibility in us. Revelation is contact with that deepest level of our psyche where archetypal wisdom rests. It also lies between the paws of the sphinx and in the words of the Sutras and Gospels. The good news is not a message from above or beyond but wells up from deep within. It is more like an underground spring that rises than like rain that falls. The equivalent of revelation in Buddhism is the dharma, the teachings of Buddha. The word "dharma" refers to the truth that is inherent in all reality. In that sense all phenomena are revelations. In "Psychotherapists or the Clergy?" Jung says:

> The living spirit grows and even outgrows its earlier forms of expression in order freely to choose the men who proclaim it and in whom it lives. This living spirit is eternally renewed and pursues its goal in manifold and inconceivable ways throughout the history of humankind. Measured against it, the names and forms which men have given it mean very little; they are only the changing leaves and blossoms on the stem of the eternal tree.

When rituals and beliefs are taken literally, they lose their meaning as inner events. We find adult faith by giving that up. There has always been a tradition of nonliterality *while* having faith, both within the Church structure and outside it. Dropping literalism is the central task in the transition from childhood belief to adult faith. How? By finding continuity with our religious past, not in its literal forms but in the experiential meaning that underlies it. This means reviving the bond we had with our religion, without having to rejoin the Church institutionally unless we wish to. We rejoin if we find a community of believers who also are freeing themselves from literalism and who offer guidance and support in our adult ways of being religious.

Here is a challenge for those who can drop the literalism of the past: the Tibetan and the Egyptian Books of the Dead give detailed information about how to prepare for death and rebirth. Perhaps the New Testament is not meant to be simply the story of Jesus. Perhaps it provides an extended metaphor about us. In that sense, it can be regarded as the Christian Book of the Dead. Sacred history is indeed the prototype of the psychic life story of every person. Phrases like "the Lamb of God," "the bread from heaven," "the way, truth, and life" are not titles of Jesus only, but titles held by him in trust for us. He was our spokesman, proclaiming our wider identity in the transpersonal world. Biblical imagery then applies to every individual. Our projections about it are the contents of our own fully realized psyches. For instance, we are meant to be alone in the wilderness and confront our destiny. The same forty days was what was required for the alchemical process and for Egyptian embalming. It is the sacred number for the passover from limitation to limitlessness, from Egypt to the Promised Land. Incarnation, kindly love, healing, crucifixion of ego, descent and ascent, rebirth: all the experiences of Christ make up the story of the Self.

> *The gods are the reflections and radiance of our own souls.*
> — CARL JUNG

Mirror Images

Since we perceive through limited senses we are innately unable to see the full extent and meaning of the divine. Faith is the complementary way humanity knows its own deepest reality. Marcus Aurelius, in *Meditations VII*, says that we find religious truths in images that arise from the depths of our souls.

Images manifest the psyche, but the psyche itself is a mystery. Images are only its trail and its products. They are clues, not portraits. Faith images point to phenomena. Yet, even if nothing happened in reality, that is, there were no original phenomenological fact, religious declarations would still be true. This is because they describe a psychic truth that does not require a logical or linear foundation. They are nonetheless supported by ancient and consistent antecedents in all traditions in all times. In other words, they describe the transhistorical, transliteral truth about us. They are the archetypal facts of life and of humankind's vision of itself, of nature, and of the divine.

"Symbol is essence and image is psychic energy," wrote Jung. A symbol is our way of conceiving the inconceivable. A true symbol not only directs us to a hidden reality but reveals that same reality in ourselves. A symbol thus creates immediate contact with the transcendent yet immanent Self. Paul Tillich says: "A real symbol points to an object that can never become an object. It points to ourselves." Religious symbols can be appreciated for their adaptive potential, a capacity to discover the core of our inner world, something deeper than anything psychological, something expressible only in symbols. Such symbol-making might not have happened without religion. Mythic art, poetry, and images indicate our capacity for depth. They are not signs of regression but of potential. Childhood religious images that comfort us are retained within us and arise later in our imagination when they are needed. Faith is actually the transcendent use of imagination.

How are potentials actualized? By imaging. Athletes who picture themselves winning are more likely to win. All our lives as Catholics we have been surrounded with images and statues. We form images in our minds as we recite the creed. Faith is an imaginative process, not an intellectual one. It thrives on images. Primordial images underlie conscious life like underground springs. They influence us, as springs, though hidden, influence the flora and fauna on the surface of the earth. Every religious image is a portrayal and blossom of some seed quality of the infinite Self. A collection of holy cards is an off-world family album. Each saint is an image of an aspect of ourselves when we are at our best. When we look at images or form them internally we are picturing our own potentials. That is the route to actualizing them. This is another example of the theme of this book: so much of our past is and was useful. It is all a matter of finding the inner pearl of great price or of believing there still is one along the journey of faith.

As Christians we were taught to worship Christ *and* to let him live within us. This comprehensive approach is universal in mature religious practice. For instance, the Buddhist practice of devotion to Avalokiteshvara, the Buddha of compassion, is fourfold: to venerate his image, to let it appear as both male and female, that is, whole, to grasp that the image is a mirror of oneself, and to act with a similar compassion in the world. (Avalokiteshvara means "the Lord who is visible from within.") The result of devoted imaging is that a "wisdom duplicate" of the god becomes detectable in us. Devotion is thus a path to self-realization. This does not minimize the divine but grants it full purchase of itself.

Authentic religion thus does not repose in adoration but opens into consciousness of inner divinity and universal love. Such indelible archetypal truths of the psyche unfurl in Catholicism, in Buddhism, and in all sincere religions and perennial philosophies. The challenge is to see how our own inner truth matches the truth of religion and then to integrate it all in daily life.

The Chinese form of the Buddha of compassion is *Kuan Yin,* a name that means "she who hears the cries of world." She was so touched by the pain of those in the hell realm that she emptied it in one moment of boundless mercy. (It was refilled in one moment to show the boundlessness of the shadow too!) Notice the striking archetypal similarity between this story and that of our Lady of Mount Carmel, the merciful patroness of those in purgatory. In fact, she was pictured with them in her icon. This was the first time the image of the Madonna included other humans, and it declared the intense and indelible commitment of heaven to earthly beings. The feminine presence of the transpersonal is a caring reality.

> *The religion of the future will be a cosmic religion. It should transcend a personal God and avoid dogma and theology....It should be based on a religious sense arising from the experience of all things natural and spiritual as a meaningful unity. Buddhism answers this description.*   — ALBERT EINSTEIN

Myths and Dogmas

The life forces of the psyche — physical, psychological, and religious — express themselves in history and in individual lives. An archetype is incomprehensible in itself. It is revealed only through its products, that is, dreams, synchronicities, religious experiences. Most dogmatic statements fail to reflect archetypal meanings which continually — never once for all — reveal themselves in here and now experience. This is why no single formulation can be set in stone. *Our faith is not in final statements of truth but in the experience of truth perennially cherished.*

Any single revelation would not honor or reflect the ongoing nature of human evolution.

Throughout human history, experience has led to documentation, which can become orthodox belief and inflexible morality. Then anyone is wrong and bad who does not follow the rules. The mystics put the accent on experience, not the dogma. This animates rather than codifies the experience of human-divine encounters. Dogma may put imagination to sleep, but an animating myth stimulates consciousness so that buried truths can arise. Then we are ready for the next experience, that is, we progress, we evolve, our God is marching on. This is a way of saying that the reality of movement is contact with the Source.

"Myth is the revelation of the divine life in man," said Jung. Revelation and myth evolve like consciousness. Dogmas, strongly held beliefs, assist us when they align with the truth of psyche. Whatever is not deeply rooted in our unconscious will feel alien. Phrases like "the bosom of Abraham" or "Vengeance is mine," or "Dash their children's heads against the rocks" present split archetypes that do not resound authentically in the psyche. Deep within we know that a man does not have a nurturant bosom, that true goodness does not retaliate or act violently. The powerful image of the Madonna lasts throughout the centuries because all of us associate nurturant motherhood with a female. The heart of Jesus appeals to us because we know instinctively and innately, that is, archetypally, that love is wounded and does not wound back. This is the heart of the Self, not the heartlessness of ego. Religion works when it taps into our mythic roots, and the psyche cannot be fooled by patriarchal biases or ego conceits.

Doctrines are only fossils when they refer to some ancient person's experience that becomes normative ever after. We can perceive doctrines more positively, not as rigid directions but as guideposts that support our personal interior search for the truth of our life. Images become idols when they no longer have the power to reflect our inner life of unconditional love, perennial wisdom, and healing power.

As we have been seeing, if revelation touches base with archetypal roots, it speaks to the depth of the psyche, the divine life awakening, the God within. This cannot easily happen in statements that are culture and time-bound or imposed from without. An adult does not confuse a theological formulation with the mysterious reality of the one psyche-God that can never be adequately described and hardly even approximated. Duns Scotus wrote: "God does not know himself what he is, because he is not a *what*. In that sense, he is as incomprehensible to himself as to any human intellect."

Dogmas and creeds seemed the only way to formulate faith in the past. The task now is not to see through doctrines but to see into them. For instance, most dogmas in Catholicism are not arbitrary papal pronouncements but represent mythologems from the faith psyche of humankind. Before Pope Pius XII pronounced the dogma of the assumption of Mary into heaven, he wrote to all the bishops of the world. He asked them what the local Catholics believed about the assumption. The overwhelming belief was that Mary was indeed assumed into heaven bodily to become the Queen of Heaven. Only then did he proclaim the dogma. Solemn beliefs are not imposed upon but elicited from the commonalty of belief already in the believing community. The community believes that way because of a long tradition. That long tradition survived because it matches the truth of the human psyche. This is how the psyche's truth come together with revelation and doctrine. As Jung says: "Revelation is an unveiling of the depths of the human soul. Every revelation is about man as well as about God."

Dogma expresses the living drama of our inner life — found in images — so to toss out the images is to lose the archetypal values they depict and proclaim. Rituals enact the initiation process, so loss of ritual is dangerous to the psyche which thrives on them. (Rituals are also a protection against forces of the unconscious — too overwhelming to face directly.) Thus religion seems necessary to the full blooming of our psychic powers. Religion is not a villain in the human story; it is an assisting force. Afflicting forces are those opposed to our awakening to these facts about ourselves. This opposition is the "flesh" referred to in the New Testament and the *samsara* of oriental religion. Assisting forces help us know and deal with the afflicting forces.

God and I

Religious experience is simply our awareness of communion with the Ultimate. Meister Eckhart call the Ultimate "God," but those who feel less comfortable with that word are certainly not barred for that reason from experiencing the reality to which the word "God" points. — BROTHER DAVID STEINDL-RAST

It is not that God is a myth but that myth is the revelation of a divine life in man. — LUCIEN LEVY-BRUHL

There is no single universal signature, only individually unique ones. There is no single love, only each person's brand in giving and receiving it. There can be no single image of God, only individual experiences of God. The word "God" has bad press today because it has a male-sounding resonance. It also sounds dualistic, as if God were a supreme separate being beyond human experience. "One God" sounds like a single entity with a perimeter. The word "God" is also controversial since it is associated with so many divergent concepts. Actually, "God" can refer to the space between the concepts of God. The issue is not whether God is but whether he is nothing but what we have heard of him literally, for instance, that he is a he! (Since devotion is so important a feature of religion, it is understandable that the terms "Father" and "Lord" were used throughout history. Devotion leads to comfort and security, and that is associated with a father or lord who protects us.)

What people have meant by God has taken many forms:

- a male spirit in the sky who sees, knows, and influences all

- a person who extends or supplements the power of our ego to punish or reward

- a principle of providential comfort

- a loving and consoling friend who helps us

- a person who hears and answers prayers and can reverse the conditions of existence

- the Trinity, Father, Son, and Holy Spirit

- a metaphor for a mystery of presence and meaning

- a guarantor of ultimate meaning or the ultimate meaning itself

- the source and destination of all

- the inner life of all things, the deepest reality of all phenomena as well as their purpose

- love (usually excluding erotic love) and a guarantee of being personally loved

- any combination of the above.

Any word signifying limit cannot account for the mystery of the infinitely expanding universe-psyche. The center of the universe is the center of us. "God" is a word for the ground of that center, the source of the center. This is another meaning of the indwelling of the Holy Spirit. In Buddhism, what we imagine to be ground is void or space. Perhaps that spaciousness can be what we mean by God. What a pivotal connection between Buddhism and Christianity: the void, the no-self, is the Self.

A galaxy revolves around an invisible, intangible center that is a still point and yet is continually moving. It is space, not form. "At the still point of the turning world ... at the still point, there is the dance," writes T. S. Eliot. There can be a center that is no-thing, as Buddha says of our identity: we are not a solid self but an inner void or space. A person is five continually changing elements that are united for a specific lifetime: body, feelings, perceptions, mental states, and consciousness. These elements are formed by interacting with others and are therefore interdependent. This is what is meant by no-self. "There is no self to be dissolved, only a notion of self to be transcended," says Thich Nhat Hanh.

It is not that there is nothing in the nihilistic sense but no-thing in the sense of no single, limiting, separate independent reality. What we call "I" is nothing but an ever shifting assembling of physical and intellectual phenomena. The universe is a dynamic harmony: "still and still moving." It is maintained by an equilibrium of attraction and repulsion: a balance of opposites. The center of ourselves is likewise still. It is a central axis point with no dimensions, like a point of light with no limits. This is how the center is everywhere and simultaneously is no thing. When that same essential being at the heart of us and of the universe is honored in itself, it is called God: the formless presence of being that is the same in every form and yet not limited to any one of them. God is the no-thing behind things, the infinite spaciousness behind the limited appearances.

The spaciousness-void is personally liberating. It is a way of declaring that our identity lies beyond any specific representations. This is what it means to be grounded. The individual self is not God, but the God within is the ground of our deepest being, related as ground to figure in art. Bernadette Roberts said: "What I called myself was the totality of being wherein God was the center." Intimacy is the feeling that comes with this realization since the sense of Self is contact with, not alienation from, the rest of humankind and the universe. This intimacy is what is called religious devotion.

A human person is one moment of being that has become aware of itself. The universe is being creating itself. God is being in itself. This equation — God is the universe is humankind — and its triune nature, cannot be known logically. Our linear mind is only equipped to know the forms being takes, not being itself since it is ineffable. There are, however, elements of the psyche that transcend space-time linearity, such as dreams, intuitions, psychic readings, and synchronicity. In mystical states or in mindfulness meditation we dissolve limiting representations and contact essential being. Meaningfulness is in that which has essential, enduring unlimited being. This is why spiritually oriented people do not see the world as meaningless, that is, having no essential being.

To affirm meaningfulness is to say there is an essential being behind even the most fragile and unpromising appearances. This divine reality has been experienced by mystics in all traditions as something preciously and exquisitely personal. To look for meaning is to look into the Self: the center and circumferencelessness of us, things, and God. The essential Self — the being of the universe, God, and us — is a triune reliable reality that is the meaning of us and of all life. That which is meaningless is pointless, but we are centered, exquisitely and graciously, in a point of unending light. Life is meaningless only when we cease letting that light through.

There can be no name for the ultimate lest it become reified and then become an object of fear or desire. This is especially contradictory and confounding since the spiritual path is about letting go of fear and desire, the sports of the ego. Our collective intrapsychic image of God may have become ego-designed and ego-motivated. The word "God" is a way of describing our vast potential for love. God within means that God is whatever in us becomes more and more conscious, more and more loving.

It is important to realize that the word "God" denotes our *experience* of the divine. It too is a metaphor for a mystery that cannot be limited by words, concepts, or even individual experiences. Nicholas of Cusa presented an allegory for God as a circular sea with no loss of water and a spring in the center that is ever surging. That does not sound limitable by concepts or dogmatic formulations. The Self, the vast psychic ego-transcending aliveness in humankind and in nature, is the experience of God. There is truly no inside vs. outside, only *fields*, as in magnetic fields.

Contact with essential identity feels like meaning, purpose, centered identity, and an intimate presence without interruption. Divine energy is thus the spiritual and inherent organizing principle of our psyche. This is the metaphor of God as the creator. Within creation is its opposite: destruction. Thus in Hinduism, the trinity consists of a creator, a preserver, and a destroyer. Since the divine is the ground of being and being involves an evolutionary rhythm of creation and dissolution, it has to include that darker possibility. God is a personification of that which transcends the collapses that characterize reality while at the same time accommodating them. God is a way of referring to that which integrates apparently disparate and opposing forces such as creation and dissolution. We were taught the three-in-one and prepared for the all-in-one. Perhaps it is time to expand our notion of the Trinity to the *Infinity*. We always believed that unity includes diversity, but it has taken us a long time to realize how much that can include.

God is the wholeness that is impelled by unconditional love, perennial wisdom, and healing power rather that compelled by fear and desire. God lives in the world by the activation of human potential. The more other-worldly God becomes, the more depreciated is the value of our potential. Incarnation is actualization of the fullest potential and farthest reach of human-divine life. If God is the eternal Self made conscious in our life and lifetime, then we are the necessary midwives for its epiphany. Revelation about God is evolving by and as the light of human consciousness, one person at a time. It all hangs on the human psyche with heart.

The vastness of the psyche is exactly congruent to the vastness of the universe. Psyche reflects cosmos. Our work is to experience something transcendent in nature and to say: "This is familiar; I felt this in the depths of myself." The meaning out there matches the felt meaning we always find within. This is how we realize that the sacred is not an object but a continually unfolding reality that reflects itself in us. We can see it as reflecting the vastness of our psyche and stop there, or we can say it has a foundation transcendent of our psyche. Both are religious statements since both acknowledge a transcendence of that which the linear mind calls real.

Meister Eckhart rewrote St. Paul's words: "Nothing can separate me from the love of God" as "Nothing can separate me from what I find within me." This fits for someone who also said: "In my breakthrough I see that God and I are one." There was always a voice of illumined mystics in and out of the Church who saw that God was not a person, a supreme being above us. In our childhood religious indoctrination we were not granted that option but were taught an incontrovertible dualism. What was thereby excluded from divinity was our own humanity. The old heresy of Monophysitism was applied to our incarnation as it was to Christ's. In addition, when holiness is only in a supreme Being over us, then natural things are depleted of their holiness and so is the psyche.

In Hinduism, liberation happens when the *atman*, the inner Self and the divine Self, are recognized as one and the same. Notice this same idea in the following words of a Western thinker, Thomas Merton:

The spark which is my true self is the flash of the Absolute recognizing itself in me. This realization at the apex is a coincidence
of all opposites . . . a fusion of freedom and unfreedom, being and
unbeing, life and death, self and nonself, man and God. The spark
is not so much an entity which one finds but an event, an explosion
which happens as all opposites clash within oneself. Then it is
seen that the ego is not. It vanishes in its nonseeing when the flash
of the spark alone *is*. . . . The purpose of all learning is to dispose
man for this kind of event. The purpose of various disciplines is
to provide ways or paths which lead to this capacity for ignition.

The True Self is the farthest reach of our potential, that is, God, the
complete articulation of the best of our humanity, the actualization of
every potential for human love, wisdom, and healing. This is not a person above us as traditional theism teaches. God is the climax of human
powers that made an appearance in Christ and keeps appearing in many
other saints. It makes an appearance in us every time we love. God's
presence is that moment of love made human in any here and now.

> *This is not God as an ontological other set apart from the cos-
> mos, from humans, and from creation at large. Rather it is God as
> an archetypal summit of one's own consciousness. . . . In this way
> only could St. Clement say that he who knows himself knows
> God, . . . a deity which from the beginning has always been one's
> own Self and highest archetype. . . . The absolute is both the high-
> est level of reality and the condition or real nature of every level
> of reality. . . . The absolute is both the highest stage or goal of evo-
> lution and the ever present ground of evolution, your real and
> present condition and your future potential. . . . All things are al-
> ready and fully Buddha just as they are. All things are already
> One or always already One, and all things are trying to evolve
> toward the One or omega point. . . . That is why you are Buddha
> but still have to practice.*
> — KEL WILBER

A Dazzling Darkness Too

At the same time, there is a dark side to this picture. The depth of
our psyche is comprised of a union of opposites. This implies that God
also contains opposites. God is the eternal light *and,* as Henry Vaughn
says, "a deep and dazzling darkness" too. The Bible gives many indications of this. The story of Job is a prime example of inflicting evil

unnecessarily. Other passages in the Old Testament also show this: Elijah butchered the priests of Baal. "Does evil befall a city unless God has done it?" (Amos 3:6). "The Lord has made everything for his own purpose, yea, even the wicked for the day of evil" (Prov. 16:4). "I make peace and create evil" (Isa. 45:5). "When Moses halted for the night, Yahweh came to meet him and tried to kill him" (Exod. 4:24). "Yahweh said, 'Who will trick Ahab into marching to his death?' " (1 Kings 22:20). The words "Lord God" have come to have an ominous sound because they indicate so much retaliatory, and therefore unforgiving, ego. The divine is that which does not give up on us not that which has to get back at us.

We were taught that God has no shadow, but mystics know better. As is so often the case, catechesis may exclude or distort what theology accommodates. Perhaps most of the archetypal truths of religion are consigned to this same sequestered silence. We deny the shadow of God because we deny the magnitude of our own human shadow. We want a God who is our refuge and our strength, a mighty fortress, not an usher to the strict conditions of existence. We fear the refuge of truth and prefer a refuge from it. This is not a reason for shame or a sign of waywardness. It is just what the ego naturally does in its own defense in a world besieged by so much suffering and uncertainty. The challenge is not to forsake any hope of refuge. The challenge is to take refuge where it can be found. It will be in the yes to light *and* shadow. This is just the chiaroscuro world in which we need to evolve as beings of depth, and in it the God of depths grants a lap but not an exemption.

The metaphor of Eden and redemption depicts a God motivated and driven by ego: God shows his shadow before Eve does; he threatens with punishment. He shows it again after the sin when he demands expiation by the death of his son. The ego God of the Old Testament follows a domination and retaliation model that was later exploited by patriarchal religion to oppose human freedom. Pluralism is an inherent human quality, the vehicle by which we expand and discover the dimensionality of truth. To crush it is to limit our creativity, our godlikeness.

It is true that God is love, but love is tough at times. Storms, earthquakes, the devouring of the weak animals by the stronger ones, destructive forces unleashed on populations are examples of nature's ruthlessness. Yet this dark side of nature makes evolution possible. The dark side of God is like that of nature; it is an afflicting force that ultimately becomes an assisting one. The inexorable and necessary conditions of existence are the shadow of God. The unity of the divine, the natural, and the human shows how the shadow of the Self operates in the world. Since the ratio includes nature, it has a destructive dimension, as does the divine, as does the human, as crime and misdeeds attest. The divine collective shadow and the human shadow joined forces for the Holocaust and Hiroshima.

The Self is indeed unconditional love, perennial wisdom, and healing power. It is enduringly luminous in those ways. At the same time, the Self has a shadow side that can be painful and dangerous. "Our God is a consuming fire," says the Book of Hebrews. There is no dualism in the divine but there is distinction, light and dark. The dark is not evil but it is destructive and it is felt as evil by us when we fail to make a full contract with the conditions of existence. The dark side of God is to be revered but not feared. It is how the wholeness of human experience, and of nature, happens.

Hell and demons are meant to be literary, not literal. The story of Eden and the devil is a poetic way of saying something about a waywardness in our human will that cannot be explained by any fault of ours. We inherited a tendency to want to do one thing and instead to do another. We make choices that lead us away from our happiness and become agents of pain to others. That psychic fact of the split between the healthy and the dysfunctional ego is told in a literary way in the Bible.

Demons are a psychological construct. Ma-Chig-La, a twelfth-century Buddhist teacher, said: "Anything that obstructs the attainment of liberation is a demon. [A savior is one who clears the path to liberation.] Demons do not literally or concretely exist. The greatest demon of them all is belief in a self as an independent and lasting entity. If you do not destroy this clinging to a self, demons will just keep lifting you up and letting you down." The Tibetan teacher Trungpa Rinpoche adds: "It is with our emotions that we create demons and gods. Those things we want out of our lives and the world are the demons; those things we would draw to ourselves are the gods and goddesses."

Demons are thus psychic fields, projections of the shadow of the collective unconscious. Buddhism succeeded in acknowledging that gods and demons do not exist in any primitive and literal way *while at the same time preserving the primal archetypal reality of the inner life they signify.* That is the ongoing and essential challenge in designing an adult Christian faith from the relics of our past.

Devils are fabrications of the ego to maintain a split and to safeguard the concept of an all-good God. Lucifer comes to be only when we deny the wholeness of God. The task of consciousness is to restore it.

God does this for himself in Book X of *Paradise Lost* when he calls
the devils "*My* hellhounds." The Old Testament quotations above are
similar indications. Religion often deals with the shadow by saying,
"Don't do that," but depth psychology says "Make it conscious and
befriend it so it becomes an ally." Can we be courageous enough to see
this as applicable also to our sense of God?

Once the shadow is restored to God, a separate hell realm is no
longer a useful metaphor. Michael P. Morrissey writes:

> Hell is the abolition of one's essential being through the failure to
> overcome the disintegration of the temporal conditions of human
> existence. The everlasting torment of hell symbolizes the total irre-
> vocable nature of self-damnation, the consequence of one's willful
> separation from the divine ground of being through the obdurate
> absorption in one's own self-interests over that of others.... In
> essence, hell is the eternal loss suffered by the refusal to love.

Religion has a shadow side as we have been seeing. One dimension of
the shadow of the Church is in its medieval history of repression and
cruel tortures of human persons. It is also dark in its use of political
alliance and intrigue to bolster its own interests. This has been a theme
in the institutional Church that continues into modern times. The collective shadow of Catholicism has to be recognized and dealt with. The
Inquisition and the Crusades are egregious and shameful examples of
the genocidal shadow of the Church. So is the genocide of street children in South America when it is connected to the Church's power to
prevent a country from passing reasonable birth control laws, and as
a result children multiply with no chance of nurturance or survival.
When will the Church ask forgiveness of humankind for its historical
and its present abuses?

The Church has a long history of light and shadow. The jubilee year
2000 celebrates the light. It would be a touching and moving moment
if the jubilee began as the Mass does, with a confession of guilt against
human freedom, human life, and human happiness. Like all confessions
it would be completed by contrition, amends, and a resolve to change.
This would be a telling revelation of how religion leads to the letting
go of ego and to a dedication to compassion.

Today we see such a poignant yearning for community. Yet community is sometimes a destructive place to be, as the comforting sense
of oneness felt in Nazi times by the German people testifies. The ego
driven by fear and grasping or by self-justification and exclusivity is
the shadow of any community. A sense of community is useful in many

ways, but it is dangerous to idealize such a solution. "When two or three are gathered in my name, I am in the midst of them," Jesus said. Yes, that is true — and his shadow may be present too.

Room for Heresy?

Heresy is often the recovery of truths
that onesidedness has rejected.

Pope John Paul II in his book *Crossing the Threshold of Hope* speaks of the Gospel as "the grand affirmation of the world and of man, because it is the revelation of the truth about God." "The truth," especially about God, is a frightening concept to people who want to think openly. What about a continuous revelation, an ever expanding truth, a set of approximations about God and us that gradually becomes ever more clear? This approach has much more room in it.

"We should not fear the truth about ourselves." This statement of the pope is an encouraging point of departure for courageous inquiry. The truth is a living experience of equipoise between the reality that faces me and the sense of it in me. This means that *truth is not a possession but a correspondence.* It is never final but "comes in and out of season," as Robert Frost says. There is no Truth but only this truth here and now at this moment on this journey. This does not exclude the eternal verities of the perennial philosophy or the enduring archetypes within the contemplations of religious people throughout the ages. It says that these truths become real and palpable only as they are authenticated in our own lives, moment by moment. Living faith does not mean finding our final resting place in permanently undoubting certitude. This would not be faith but fixation. True faith mirrors life; it keeps moving onward, a heroic journey, an evolution from light to dark and back to light again.

To be a Catholic can no longer mean subscribing to a list of propositions or adherence to a creed. Heterodoxy grants room — we grant ourselves room — to follow unusual paths. Catholics do not have to be attached to any single view but can be open to constant input from many sources. Combining Eastern and Western sources is especially beneficial. Sincere and continual search is what makes us Catholic, not assenting to something exactly as someone told us it was supposed to be.

In all these speculations we find a refreshing latitude of opinion about God and revelation. All through the Christian era, Catholics have been thinking in creative and imaginative terms. For centuries, this was dangerous, and many people were persecuted and even put to death for their eccentric beliefs. When Catholicism had its chance to rule, blood flowed. Today there is the same wide spectrum of belief among Catholics. The conservative churchmen still silence some of those who speak up publicly. Yet we can proclaim our freedom to believe as is phase-appropriate to our life transitions. Any sincere perspective about who God is can be a legitimate option for any Catholic. It is time to take back free speech as a religious right. Any Catholic can have any view since our views are always evolving. Catholicism is not a destination but a journey.

The mystery of the divine life is developing in our collective human consciousness, so why not in each individual consciousness too? In Buddhism and in self psychology it is clear that there is no solid, personal, distinct, substantial, underlying self in us. We may ask how there can be a personal God, a distinct supreme being, in the traditional sense in the light of those views. What we have seen so far in this book, perhaps what endures behind all appearances, human and natural, is the Infinite Self that is pure spaciousness, an inner sky. It is not that God does not exist but that the traditional way we learned about God was mostly designed by a self-protective and limiting ego. Mystics were always saying no to that and to the concept of God as a person, a supreme being above us. They experienced a oneness in God, nature, and ourselves. *Thus to be devoid of separate existence really means that all is interrelated.*

In Catholicism and in all religions there are always two forms of belief: an official view and a popular view. The popular view is usually heretical. (Elaine Pagels defines heresy: "Christian sources not endorsed by clerical authorities.") Heresies contain some truth, but are often one-sided and antihuman, for example, the Monophysitism, Pelagianism, and Manicheism discussed earlier. Others balance a one-sidedness in official teaching. The former are dangerous to wholeness; the latter enhance it. A sane and helpful heresy is a correction, not a deviation.

Heresies can be inflexible or flexible. An inflexible person with fixed ideas that run counter to the teachings of the Church is a heretic who is outside the Church. There is no dialogue possible. But there are those who are sincere seekers and have a perspective that is contrary to official Church teaching yet remain in the Church because they are still engaging in a dialogue within the Church. In this book, I am proposing that such heterodoxy is a legitimate way of being a Catholic. As long as we remain flexible and dialogical, seeing our beliefs as preliminary and provisional in our ongoing search for truth, we are in the human community of faith. It may sound like this: "Here is how I see it now, and I know this can be a phase en route to something more mature. I am open to dialogue. I am not rigid and attached to my ideas but want to learn more and am always ready to alter my opinions. Let's keep talking." This reflects the words of *Paradise Lost,* Book IX: "opener mine eyes...dilated spirits, ampler heart, and growing up."

Heresy, strictly speaking, presupposes an orthodoxy that maintains a rigid codification of belief. What is referred to as heresy may actually be heterodoxy. Heterodoxy challenges orthodox opinions. It does not oppose belief but acknowledges its immense variety. Heterodoxy can be a loyal opposition. It rejects the existential articulations of dogma while still maintaining the essential truths of religion. This kind of heterodoxy accepts and includes, unlike inflexible heresy.

In *The Shaking of the Foundations,* Paul Tillich goes one step further and proposes that if the truth has set us free we are objects of it, not seekers of it. He speaks of victory over attachment to law. Jesus Christ came to release us from the Law. The Law is rigid dogma and anti-human moral injunctions. Religion based on Law is the yoke he came to free us from. It is an easy yoke because it is not based on obedience to man-made laws but accesses an acceptance, always and already in us. "Jesus is not the creator of another religion, but the victor over religion. He is not the maker of another law but the conqueror of law.... He is the end of religion, above Christianity and non-Christianity."

Catholic Christians today have beliefs that cut across a wide spectrum. One can believe that Jesus is the unique and only Son of God. One can also believe that the Gospel message is a living metaphor of our human-divine potential. Then Jesus is the firstborn of many brethren, the exemplar of our virtues as humans who love. Jesus then does not have to be venerated as other than us in nature or being but a person like us who showed us our destiny and articulated our calling. (A calling is a hearkening to the Self rather than the ego.)

The archetypal life of Christ is a mirror of and a call to our own destiny. In the Gospel, it is hard to distinguish concrete and mythic. Christ lived a daily life of specific events and an archetypal life with mythic themes. Faith is about this latter part. Since archetypes are the stuff of our unconscious, the truth about Christ is the truth about us. He prefigures our spiritual life. We too are historical and transhistorical, simultaneously our living selves and the ongoing life of the entire human species. Deep down, we always knew ego was not all there was to us.

In our time, we have free speech and free thought and can believe as we see fit. This latitude in believing is not the official *de jure* sanctioned teaching of the Church. It is not even acceptable to most liberal theologians. But it is a *de facto* reality and always has been. People have always had their own version of the creed no matter what they said aloud at Mass. It is time to acknowledge that and grant it legitimacy. It takes courage to be a Catholic with one's own beliefs, and there has never been so much support for it as in our day.

In *Art of the Renaissance* by Peter Murray, we see Piero della Francesca's magnificent painting of the Resurrection showing Christ with one foot on the edge of his open sarcophagus: "the sleeping soldiers slump uneasily pointing to the contrast between unawakened humanity and the effulgent moment of salvation that passes unheeded." In the Gospels, it is recorded that only a few people saw the risen Christ. This is a metaphor for how few people see the deeper reality of their own religion. That happens when we think and learn from many sources and not so much when we ask one church what to believe in and stick to that all our lives. Since truth is beyond time, timely forms are provisional and only approximate. Rigid dogma cannot be right for all time when it emerges from time-bound paradigms. The truth cannot be limited by truths that are tied to time. At the same time, a formless truth cannot be fastened down in dogmatic forms: "Go not outside, return into yourself: truth dwells in the interior man," wrote St. Augustine. When archetypal truths are pinned down and rigidly formulated, they lose their richness and we lose our chance to find the riches of our faith-heritage, the "many-splendored thing."

> *Your own consciousness, shining, void, and inseparable from the Great Body of Radiance, has no birth, no death, and is the Immutable Light.*   —*Tibetan Book of the Dead*

How Religion Is about Wholeness

What, you ask, was the beginning of it all?
Existence multiplied itself for sheer delight of being.
It plunged into numberless trillions of forms
So that it might find itself innumerably.

— SRI AUROBINDO

Religion is the human response to the sacred expressed in four major ways: belief, morality, ritual, and devotion. The word "religion" is related to two Latin words: *religare,* which means to tie or fasten back, and *religere* which mean to gather up. We are joined to the source of ourselves again and again in every human experience. We are gathered, made coherent, our energies enlisted in an experience of unity. This does not happen when all we have is what William James called: "second-hand religion." It happens when we personally and concretely acknowledge a legitimate and enduring religious instinct in our psyche. We then activate its great potential to open and complete us. The fuller meaning of life is in that which transcends it.

Religious language was invented because it best describes the intrapsychic realm, that which is "written in the heart." Only religion presents the vocabulary of the unconscious: soul, divinity, spirit, resurrection, ascension, new life, initiation. The word "God" is a personification that describes the transcendent nature of the Self. God is the experience of God. Sacraments are rituals of initiation. Only religious images come close to reflecting the ineffable riches of the psyche. How could we know the touching and consoling beauty of divine love for us with only scientific words in our lexicon? Some of us require images, metaphors, and poetic forms to approach the mystery of how the divine life wants to nurture us with itself and nurture itself in us.

The enduring psychic truth underlying and suffusing religious statements is not historically bound. A reliable theology or psychology is

117

one that honors archetypal perennial wisdom as its foundation. This
fund of wisdom not contributed to by us is open to us, its heirs. Our
psyche retains its ancient gifts, wisdom, and healing powers from primordial times. In the archetypal depths of the psyche is an experience
that is one and the same as that described by religion. This wisdom is
infallible. We will always be drawn by the irresistible appeal of the light
both within and beyond us. Perennial wisdom includes such affirmations as these: all is evolving in a harmonious way; behind appearances
is something alive and mysterious that cannot be born or die; there is
no dualism; the divine life is the fulfillment of human life.

The treasury contains not only wisdom but love and healing. Every
time someone is touched by the human dilemma or acts heroically or
performs the works of mercy, a contribution is made to the fund from
which we draw our strength to do likewise. We also draw from it in moments of despair. We may feel a healing presence or discover a healing
image in a dark time. That is a gift from the storehouse of all the times
that humans acted in accord with divine nature. The gifts come to us
unsought sometimes and at other times are given in response to prayer.
The qualities of divinity are the currency of the treasury of graces. Loving people are the depositors. All of us are the beneficiaries. This is
what is meant by the repository of merits in the communion of saints.

Human individuality is thus holographic. Anything personal represents and contributes to the collective. Each of us, by our work on
ourselves, our practice, and our spiritual progress advances the consciousness of all humanity. This means that we do not have to be
members of a church community but can follow a personal path and
still be affiliated with the Church. This book is about how we can
belong without formal or visible membership. The Church is humanity in the service of the Self. When we find or create a community
that acknowledges and fosters that truth, we can be its members
enthusiastically. The choice is always ours.

Here is an example of how personal work has collective merit. As I
let go of my retaliatory ego, the world is less likely to be so punitive in
its reactions to world conflicts. Since all of us are one mystical body,
there is no such thing a solitary gesture, for good or evil. Nor is there
a collective world work that stands on its own. Individuals of faith
and love evolve personally and collectively simultaneously. This is a
profound implication of the Bodhisattva vow.

The metaphor of the transcendent treasury refers to the point of
meeting of the individual and the collective ego, of past resources and
present needs, of personal and transpersonal energies. Rupert Shel-

drake's theory about morphogenetic fields reflects this idea. The species mind — cosmic intelligence — remembers and makes its past awakenings available in the present. A whole greater than individual parts is in direct contact with each of us.

Our personal life anguish is resolved as we attend to it. Perhaps, in the bargain, the anguish of the world is thereby somewhat healed also. There is then no individual death-rebirth; it becomes collective every time and at the same time. All humanity mediates to us and we to it by a continual transfer and release of psychic energy. This includes nature, which tells its gospel in every season and in every dying, rising rose.

The universe has an integrative and teleological intelligence that directs eco-systems in their evolution. There are fields of energy in the structures of the universe that allow parts to be mediated to the whole and past to be directed to future. This is the postulation of such scientists as J. E. Lovelock ("Gaia hypothesis"), Fritjof Capra, David Bohm, and Richard Tarnas. The soul of the world is that something more expansive than any individual part and at the same time that of which every individual is a part. It heals, renews, and re-creates itself continuously. One of the forms of the Buddha is the Medicine Buddha, whose teaching is that all things in the universe have healing power in some way. Since healing is a quality of the Self this is another way of saying that all of nature is the Self. David Palmer, founder of chiropractic, spoke of the "innate intelligence" of the body. Later he became aware of the "universal intelligence" in nature, and finally he realized that both of these are one and the same. These are all striking ways to describe the triune equation of the human, divine, and natural. "Does a dog have Buddha nature?" has found an answer. Who is Christ or Buddha is the same question as who am I when my ego is not in control. Christ consciousness, Buddha mind, the Self are *ch'I*, the life force of ourselves and of the universe. *Ch'I* is the link in the ratio of oneness: human, natural, divine. Perhaps divinity may be described as in Alcoholics Anonymous: the Good Orderly Direction in everything human and natural.

Nature is consciousness made visible. It follows that the work of each individual is also the work of the universe. All of nature is finding its way to love, wisdom, and healing. The yearning in us for wholeness is the same as that of the universe and happens in the same way, by the expanding of consciousness. The species psyche evolves as the individual psyche does, taking turns at influencing each other. Here are some examples: The Western world enacts child labor laws. Individuals become aware of their inner child issues including early abuse. Individuals recognize the need for community with all humanity. The United Nations comes into being.

Perhaps our personal ego death-rebirth process is mirrored by the universe too, as St. Paul states: "all creation groans until now" for wholeness. The sufferings of humankind over the centuries and the ravages of the planet may all be part of the universe's way of the cross to Easter. "There are tears in things. . . . Perhaps someday it will help to remember all this," says Virgil, contemplating the pain and its redemptive path.

Our personal practice is what makes it happen. Not only a woman touched the hem of Jesus' garment but all humankind did too and with the same healing result. The practice is to go through our ego deaths in relation to the death of the world. We are not alone in our agonies or ecstasies. The heroes are all those who have recognized the universality of suffering and have grasped how their stories are history. The heroes have discovered the redemptive value of the struggle phase of the journey. They know they are not in this world for themselves. Their narrow ego concerns have faded in that all-embracing commitment.

An ineradicable and core yearning in the psyche wants religion because only in its unique vocabulary, rituals, and enduring beliefs is the wisdom of the ages reflected, preserved, and advanced. The outlandish and improbable declarations religion proposes thus endure throughout the centuries since they reflect an inner truth we both possess and are not ready to know fully, since the tool we use, our thinking mind, is too limited for the hugeness of the truth involved. Faith does not make the impossible possible but reveals what was always the reality. Faith makes the unthinkable fathomable, the impossible ordinary.

Once faith becomes adult it is the main contributor to our release from the Newtonian and Cartesian limitations we inherited. Our original faith endorsed those dualisms. Now we can have the faith of the mystics that cuts through it. In addition, now we have science joining us. Now we have permission to open the treasure trove of the East and see how it was always with us in this recognition of human, natural, and divine oneness.

In the depths of the psyche, sacred meanings are revealed. The inmost core of ourselves is Sinai, the locus of revelation. That interior essence is impervious to death or disfigurement. Eventually we find the indestructible diamond Self that has survived the decades of our life and the millennia of the world's life. This is what is meant by "God is eternal." Milton says in Book VI of *Paradise Lost:* "The steadfast empyrean shook throughout, / All but the throne itself of God." That throne is the Self firmly standing in us no matter how much the ego quakes.

> *My beloved is the mountains, the lonely wooded valleys, strange islands, resounding rivers, the whistling of love-stirring breezes, the tranquil night at the time of the rising dawn, silent music, sounding solitude, and the supper that refreshes and deepens love.*
> — ST. JOHN OF THE CROSS, *Spiritual Canticle*

The Religious Instinct

Religion survives for the same reason that anything survives, because it serves a function, as Darwin would say. Religion is the limited ego's response to limitlessness since it recommends reverence toward powers beyond its control. A religious attitude toward our inner life is a reverence for ourselves as tabernacles of the divine. The Ark of the Covenant, the Eucharist, the Grand Canyon, and the human soul are all one reality. Religion thus serves to preserve the supremacy of the Self and to locate it in nature and in our human selves: the Song of Songs is a passionate celebration of this triune ratio since it tells of human love in metaphors of nature and does not mention God by name. There is no need. The divine is understood when the human and the natural are present in full color.

The religious attitude toward the world includes a trust in an immortally loving intent behind every twist of fate. Such trust evokes an unconditional yes to the conditions of existence. It also helps us access and express our unique gifts. Creativity, for example, is an existential capacity, a response to a force that taps on any shoulder. It is not simply a trait of some special people. When religion taps us that way, it becomes a key to becoming who we *fully* are. This is how the religious attitude leads to and contributes to individuation — now perceived as world individuation.

Ken Wilber writes: "Religion is a science of spiritual experiences." Adult religion is not about superstitions or postulations to believe in. It is a call to activate our wide range of powers. Beliefs are meant to be road signs to acting lovingly, wisely, and helpfully in the face of life's conditions by contributing the rich expanse of our unique potential to the world's woes and challenges. This is how religion is a useful, legitimate, and necessary part of evolution.

The religious instinct is not an epiphenomenon of the brain but new research shows that the inclination toward religion and its rituals are located in a specific brain center. We did not learn to be religious. We are religious by nature. Religion is as deeply imprinted in human nature as the instinct for survival. In 44,000 B.C., a cave dweller left hyacinths on the grave of a friend. The pollens remained with the excavated bones and were found recently. Something untaught in the human heart always believed in the transcendence of death, that is, in something behind appearances. A religious instinct in us always believed that rituals made contact with that something. The hyacinth that came back to life from the grave in which it was laid must have given the clue to the rebirth potential of both natural and human death. The divine was perhaps suspected to be the mediating force that fostered such resurrections. Perhaps the triune ratio was budding in the spiritual gardens of our first parents.

The sacred and the profane were not antagonists in the past. Psychological and religious experiences were all one. The split between them happened when healing first lost its connection to religion and entered the realm of science. As whole beings, our psychology cannot be separated from our religious instinct, that is, our inclination to design beliefs, morality, rituals, and devotion as our response to intimations of the divine. A soulful psychology unifies and protects the personal and unique quality of our religious responses. A soulful psychology is one that acknowledges that religion is necessary to the full structuring of the human psyche. Our psychological work and our spiritual practices coalesce in this process. This is how religion is the missing link between the personal and the transpersonal.

Our sense of ourselves as whole means we have interior psychological, spiritual, and religious dimensions to be explored and accessed in the course of our lives. It is hard to imagine us fulfilling ourselves just with what psychology offers or just with what religion offers. Spiritual practices do not address the issues that have to be worked out emotionally. Psychology has little to say to us when we feel the need to place hyacinths on a grave. Religion may not help us get over a phobia. Each area is insufficient of itself. Yet all three dimensions become useful and adequate in a synergistic way if we access and integrate them all. Our childhood religion probably did not show us how to find what religion can really offer us, as Freud did not give us all that psychology can offer. It is our work to expand our experience of each of the dimensions of ourselves and to design a paradigm that works for us today. We are not alone in this. Many people today are working in all three areas. We have resources we never had before. The religion of our childhood could have been a major resource. Unfortunately, most of us learned to take the most unfathomable truths of religion in literal ways and to codify its most precious values in superficial or inflexible rules. That reduced the appeal of religion as a resource. This can be reversed and recast more personally, relevantly, and passionately.

The sacred is always the ground of human experience, so psychological man is religious man. The inner self is the divine Self. This is an interiorly mature realization. True religion is founded in a fearless nondualism. It is not fear and awe of the Fearsome Other but a dawning awareness that there *is* no other. This mystery is so awesome that the power it points to *seems outside* us. The sense of otherness is a metaphor of that transcendence but the reality remains nondual. Nondual does not mean that all reality is one as opposed to many. It means that reality combines opposites; it is both one and diverse, both permanent and passing, both separate and united, both timebound and timeless.

The Buddha of compassion, Bodhisattva Amitabha, lives in a paradise in the west that has the capacity to hold all humanity. He is the horseman of and escort to enlightenment with a longing to bring all beings into the light of conscious love. Yet his paradise is everywhere, the catholic everything within reach.

Evolution not only happens in us but through us. We are responsible for it. Love is the way this happens between us. It joins us at the deepest level, the interior essence in which human and divine are facets of one mysterious presence — our mindful presence here and now. In the excellent film *Contact* a character says that all we have is each other. That places a cosmic cargo on an individual-size ship. We seem to require something more to sustain us than one another. If there is nothing more, this whole human experiment is a joke: we were made with requirements that cannot be filled; we were made with longings that cannot be fulfilled. Yet, the archetypal images in the psyche stand by for us. They suggest the possibility both in us and around us of forces that fulfill us beyond the merely human. Human nature was formed with the capacity for hypostatic union; hence incarnation is possible: the divine life lived in individual lives. Our destiny is to display in time the timeless design of the universe. We are supported in that by something well-disposed toward us and ever present at the core of our being. This is also what is meant by God as love. And when we love, there is a God.

The religious instinct is precisely what so many of us have denied to our children when we reared them with no religious affiliation. That word "affiliation" means joined as a son or daughter. We joined them to ourselves but not to the larger parental Source of the universe-Self.

This makes the formation of a coherent sense of a spiritual Self difficult for them because something seems to be missing. It is not our fault. We thought we were preserving them from the abuses, mind control, and repression of our own religious past. If only we had kept the baby when we threw out the bath water. If only we had found a way to retain the archetypal riches and rituals without the rest of it. Further, how much of what we "saved" them from was fear of their or our own religious potential, with all its illogical and uncontrollable fire so scary to the logical ego?

Individuation and Incarnation

When we find joy and divinity in our humanity,
we have found the meaning of the Incarnation.

The Self is a unitary consciousness. It has also been called the Mind of God, the Buddha Mind, Big Mind, the Transpersonal Self. We live in relationship to a life and consciousness larger than any single ego can contain. The Self is the same in all of us. Each of us breathes in slightly different rhythms, yet the air is the same in all of us and in all of nature.

The Self is present in us by virtue of our birth. In the traditional view, we are sinful by birth and require baptism to reach our full spiritual stature. Perhaps in a more generous perspective, baptism is not so much necessary as *helpful*. The sacraments are enactments of the life cycle of the Self in human beings and through their initiations.

Jesus integrates features of divinity that seemed inaccessible to humans before. For example, he shows love instead of retaliation. He teaches the art of egoless love. Thus the experience of the divine Self-beyond-ego is healing because it unites friends and enemies. The arrogant ego divides the seamless garment of the Self like the soldiers at the foot of the cross dividing the vesture of Jesus. The Self lets seamlessness, nondual love, last.

Spiritual work is about how to maintain love, wisdom, and healing power in the face of any predicament rather than by reacting with defense and avoidance, the armorings of ego. The work of individuation is to build a healthy ego and to dismantle the neurotic ego. The Resurrection is the archetype that represents the transformation of consciousness from centering in the ego to centering in the Self.

Instinct is how the animals realize the Self. Standing presence is how the mountains realize the Self. Waves are how the ocean does; shining is how the sun and moon and stars do it. Conscious love is how we humans do it. This activates the potential of the Self in and through us. The rest of nature has no goal; it is already and always doing exactly what it needs to, except when we interfere. Plato in the *Timaeus* says that wisdom is harmonizing our movements with the movement of the stars.

The incarnation of Christ as Jesus is the pivot of Christianity. The will to incarnate the divine Self in the ego is an ancient theme in all traditions. There have always been beliefs that a god descended to earth to restore order or open a new path, for example, Greek myths, Krishna in the *Bhagavad Gita:* "Whenever sacred duty decays and chaos prevails, then, I create myself." A quantum leap in spiritual consciousness in human history happens as a result of just such an incarnation.

This does not have to happen in one historical moment, once for all. Jung spoke of a continuous incarnation. Our work is to incarnate in the world the virtues of the divine Self. This is described in the Annunciation when the Holy Spirit brought Jesus to Mary physically. At Pentecost, the Holy Spirit brought Jesus' message to life in Mary and the disciples evangelically, making them apostles of the word. This is a metaphor of our personal spiritual evolution: in individuation the holy spirit of grace makes it possible to access the wealth of the Self, and it is up to us to embody it in the world. Religion is about how that happens to us physically and evangelically. We are given a lifetime to do the work. We are here to open in time the timeless riches of the Self. This is why there is time.

Individuation is the psychological version of incarnation. Incarnation of the Self happens in three areas: feeling, body, and image. It happens in feelings when they are expressed sincerely, appropriately, and compassionately. Since the body is the psyche at a higher density and matter is the form consciousness takes when it enters our senses, it too has an incarnational direction. The Self incarnates into the body by feelings and into the psyche by images. To be an individual is, in fact, to be an individualization of the Self.

The divine Self thus acts via human feelings, needs, values, and wishes. When we live in accord with our deepest needs and values and wishes, we are incarnating the Self. This helps us understand how the psychological and spiritual are indeed one: the Self incarnates as needs are fulfilled. Personal needs are spiritual needs since their fulfillment leads to wholeness, a sacred marriage of all our parts. All work is thus spiritual since we are a unity and our whole being is affected by growth in any area. This means that following our bliss is letting the light of divinity into our world. It is Pentecost.

"The glory of God is the human person fully alive," wrote St. Irenaeus. Our aliveness is enhanced by our struggle to release our full potential. Our full potential is full enlightenment, that is, full activation of the love, virtuousness, wisdom, and healing power we see in the saints. The Incarnation proclaims that this world is the best-equipped stage for human evolution toward enlightenment. In Buddhism, Pure Land refers to any place where enlightened beings create a milieu that fosters enlightened living. This is also a definition of the Church. The Church is happening wherever sincere people are progressing toward incarnation, that is, enlightenment, and sharing it as the good and healing news, as the disciples did on Pentecost. The ultimate meaning of nonduality is this: "I am part of all and essential to all. My faithwork is the same as my individuation and is the same as my work of building the world." This is how individuation is to the individual what eschatology is to collective humanity.

Our concern when we are spiritually mature is not whether or how we survive after death. It is that we live in eternity right now and may fail to notice it. Our consciousness contains something beyond mortality. Behind the appearance of limitation is something larger than any of our dimensions. The human soul is the bridge between time and eternity. We live where the opposites meet. This is why the Incarnation is so apt a way of describing who we really are. The soul is the center and foundation of the psyche. It is like the center of the labyrinth where Ariadne waits to bring liberating wisdom to the ego-driven Theseus. History is full of tales about the rendezvous between ego and Self.

As long as incarnation is the style of individuation, we face the same problems and conundrums that God faces: why do the innocent suffer, etc. Becoming human-divine means becoming accountable. This is how we are all guilty of the Holocaust. Questions beginning with why make less and less sense. The more conscious we become, the fewer questions remain and the larger the mystery. Faith indeed happens when we live with a question long enough that it becomes a longing and then, at last, a cry. That cry is prayer, the completion of faith.

To individuate is to relate to the archetypes and integrate their energies into our life experience. Mystics do not identify with God but relate to God in so close a way that union results. The work of incarnation-individuation is not to identify the coherence of our identity with a personal god but to relate them as compatible, like the image of me in a mirror vs. me myself. Rapprochement leads to unity. Twoness and oneness is universal in human experience. "The truth of being and of nothing is the unity of the two. This unity is becoming," says the mystical philosopher Hegel.

An encounter with the infinite Self can feel fragmenting because in it our patchwork life is challenged so cogently. A sense of the Self may call into question every belief and technique we have been using to hold our life together. The divine touches us at the heart of our deepest vulnerability. Only there is the opening into which healing can be poured and in which true cohesion with the Self can happen. *Do I cling to the beliefs because of this fear of fragmentation? Is faith for me only a port in the storm of life's uncontrollable conditions? What is the question to which my faith is an answer?* True faith is a vessel continually at sea. How do we deal with the unconscious without fragmenting? The Self, personified in Jesus, is the savior saving us from fragmentation. Jung saw active imagination as a path to integration. Therapy contributes since it provides a container in which fragmentation and recollection can happen safely and developmentally. Since these are opposites, we know their destiny is union. Spiritual practice brings us to the serene and sane space where divisions disappear and the psychological work shifts to a higher gear. Everyone is a Christopher, not just one incarnation but a continuum of incarnation of all humankind. A human being is a moment in which the transpersonal has become personal. Incarnation is an appearance that creates transparence.

The Pivot of Wholeness

Individuation is twofold. It means personal wholeness. It means continual extension into the world to gather all beings to the all-embracing Self. Compassion is essential to full individuation. Individuation creates contact with the source of archetypal energy in the Self within us. The return to the loving Source refers to this inward journey to the still-point Self by the ego. The ego then cycles out again to all humankind in lovingkindness. The centrifugal pivot that redirects us back from the Source to the world requires a power beyond our ego. That gift from the psyche is called grace. Grace is the pivot in fact.

The spiritual journey is thus a circular one. It walks us through the labyrinth to the center, which is a pivot turning us back out again. This is the ancient theme of ascent and descent. To ascend is to leave ego behind and enter the world of the Self; to descend is to return to the world of ego with the gifts of the Self. To descend is also to plumb the depths of the underworld, the unconscious that establishes continuity with our ancestors. The ascent-descent theme is a celebration of the marriage of life's central opposites: mortal ego and deathless Self. Not to experience the divine in the human is to lose faith. To identify the divine with the human is possession by faith. To honor the divine is devotion.

The origin and goal of our experience of God is in the pivotal point in the inner life of the psyche. It can be described as a pilgrimage to a shrine. The opportunity for grace draws us to it. Once we are there we realize we cannot stay there forever in awe of the enshrined saint or god. We find ourselves standing at a pivot of grace that faces us back to the world. We say yes to that new direction, and we are mediators of grace to the world that waits for us. This happened to the disciples on Mount Tabor when they wanted to stay and bask in the glory of the Self but were reminded of their tasks in the world below. Tabor is a pivot, not a hearth.

The old word for shrine is "fane." Fanatics are those who cannot leave a shrine or temple. Fanatics are those who do not pivot but stay stuck in awe of the enshrined image. Fanatics diminish their destiny because they project their own powers onto the saint in the shrine and are content to leave them there. When we withdraw projections we discover the universal accessibility of the powers we were in awe of. All the unconditional love, perennial wisdom, and healing powers are revealed to be within us once we cease our projecting. The mystery of Christ and the Incarnation happens in all of us. In ancient Egypt, the Pharaoh was worshiped as the only one who could be fully saved. In more mature religious reflection, salvation and eternal life were acknowledged as open to all initiates, all who were willing to go beyond ego. We have arrived at the consciousness of the mature Egyptians. The "good news" is that we have recognized divine powers in humanity.

Ongoing incarnation, the essence of individuation, means that we keep appropriating the gifts of the Self into our sense of our own identity and into our life choices. Dialogue between the ego and the Self is not possession of one by the other, as in projection, or animosity of one toward the other, as in bitterness. The Self recruits the ego many times in the course of life for its dynamic and miraculous purposes. Anyone who makes the journey is humanity's redeemer and mediates the lively energies of freedom from fear and limit.

The journey of the Self into consciousness, impelled by grace, is imaged in the Divine Child, the symbol of the pivotal point of birth: what has developed within now emerges into the outside. What has found perfect containment chooses to journey out to perfect relatedness. All are invited and included. This is why there are Jewish shepherds and gentile Magi attending Christ's birth. Likewise the birth of Moses happens between Hebrews and Egyptians, all of whom were meant to hear his message one day. All are included in his redemptive relationships. *Consciousness culminates in communion.*

Christ is not separate from the human psyche. The Christ figure is the archetype of incarnation. This is not a historical once and for all act that produces redemption and is then dispensed by the Church through the sacraments. The means of grace are in the Self and are found whenever the ego acts in service to it by unconditional love. The "Holy Spirit" refers to the activating principle of this divine love. "Salvation" means recovering and uncovering the divine life that was always ours by virtue of our humanity. Salvation is thus an awakening to what is already and always the case. It is not a new realization to arrive at but a trust in that which is immemorially grasped and cherished in the Self. It is articulation of our own truth.

Imitation of Christ is not resemblance to a historical figure but living out the archetypal truths about humanity and their challenges in his human story. His divine story is the same as ours: love, wisdom, and healing power at the price of the suffering and death of ego. The point of religion is birth and rebirth. The point of the religious search is to find the ineradicable truth of the unity of humanity with divinity. Reconciling apparent opposites *is* rebirth-resurrection.

Religious experience is what the archetypal energies of the Self feel like when they land on human consciousness. Religious experience is the impact of the Self on the ego, the impact of love on selfishness. The ego is not identical to the Self: Christ does not say: "I am the Father" but "I and the Father are one." The image is of unity, not identity. As Jung said: "We are not God, but we are the only stable in which he can be born." This mystical consciousness was marginalized throughout Church history, never truly trusted, though St. Bonaventure asserted that all Christians are called to mysticism. A patriarchal Church prefers a dualistic model in which a dependency on external sources is the only legitimate option. A human being never can grow up in such a fear-based milieu. The divine milieu was in us from the beginning. The divine is uninterrupted humanness. A personal relationship to God is contact with that boundless conscious energy that bypasses the interruptions of ego. Those interruptions are fear and the desire for more than the All we already are.

Traditional Christianity deified the masculine in opposition to the feminine, the good in opposition to the shadow, the spiritual in opposition to the material, the supernatural in opposition to the natural. We find the God that includes all these oppositions in our inner Self. There we locate the anima, the shadow, the power of nature, and our own bodies. God is the union of opposites, not the division of them. If there is a God, there is no devil.

These realizations call for the repentance of the Church for suppression of so many sincere human voices in the course of history, for the denial of power to women, for the pain caused couples by prohibition of birth control and divorce, by nonoptional celibacy, by anti-gay injunctions, and by imperialism and alliances with imperialists all through history. If this is the same Church that goes back to the time of Christ, then repentance by it is appropriate and necessary.

> *Our basic core of goodness is our true self.... The acceptance of our basic goodness is a quantum leap in our spiritual journey. God and our true self are not separate. Though we are not God, God and our true self are the same thing.*
>
> — THOMAS KEATING

Divinity Within or Above?

> *Everywhere, both east and west alike, is the Land of the Lotus Paradise. The entire universe in all directions, not a pinpoint of earth excepted, is none other than the great primordial peace ... of Buddha's Dharma-body. It pervades all individual entities, erasing all their differences, and this continues forever.... It is all a single ocean of perfect unsurpassed awakening. As such it is also the intrinsic nature of every human being.... There is no such thing as a buddha-body ... south and north, east and west, everywhere is the buddha-body in its entirety ... Buddha means "one who is awakened." Once you have awakened, your own mind is buddha. If a person wants to find buddha, he must look into his own mind, because it is there and nowhere else that buddha exists.*
>
> — ZEN MASTER HAKUIN

The word "God" may be a stumbling block to many because of its hierarchical, masculine, and dualistic associations. It can also be a useful metaphor for the ultimate, that is, that which transcends our limited egos. Traditionally, faith has meant belief that God is both transcendent and immanent. This book cannot answer the question about whether God is simply an experience from within our psyche or an independent reality that transcends the psyche. That is not in the realm of psychology or spirituality. It is a matter of how we hold our faith. Faith can encompass any sincere, personally evolving sense of the divine, be it intrapsychic or extrapsychic.

The bias of this book is in favor of the intrapsychic view since the psyche is the sole organ of experience and so it has to be present at all events of life no matter how transcendent. Yet intrapsychic does not mean fabricated. To say that the locus and origin of the divine is intrapsychic does not mean that it emanates from the human brain but that the human psyche is a tabernacle that both holds and opens. Plotinus describes it: "It is in no one place and there is nowhere it is not." All this has been preserved and expounded in Christian mystical thought, Jungian psychology, and Eastern religions, three assisting forces on the spiritual journey.

Angels are metaphors for our spiritual assisting forces. Demons personify the afflicting forces. Gabriel is a way of presenting the inner force that tells us about the path. Michael is the power that defends us on it. Raphael is the force that heals us along it. Lucifer is the shadow in us and in the world that can make the path perilously full of wrong turns and surprising hazards.

Psyche is not limited to the cranium. Intrapsychic means omnipsychic. Psyche in that context is understood as inclusive of every human being and of all the universe: "heaven *and earth* are full of your glory." Soul is not limited to humans. The world "soul" is a metaphor for how all of nature has consciousness and meaning. Meaning does not have to be configured as simply a device of the human mind. All the world is making meanings too. The world is not inferior to or in the service of humanity. Psyche and cosmos are equals continually seeking a sacred marriage. The marriage metaphor includes two universally central religious themes: the combination of opposites and the commitment to wholeness. This is why there is a ratio, an equation of interrelatedness, among the human, the natural, and the divine, one single continuum of consciousness. Thus we can say that the Sistine Chapel is a painting of what in words is *Paradise Lost,* of what in music is the Bach B-minor Mass, of what on the map is the Island of Kauai.

It is now perhaps clear that we have an interactive psyche: a personal soul and a world soul. It takes both to make a richly complete human experience. There can be no inner life separate from the natural world. Likewise the world is continually influenced by our inner life. In the communion of saints there is no personal work done or left undone. All of us are at the effect of each of us. This applies to us in nature too. We have a larger life than ego or our past or even the past of our species: we are in a world soul. The Absolute is not separate but infinitely related to us and all of nature. Our being is not an individual unit but part of an ecology. We are autonomous and related within the world soul. The reality of a world soul means there is no objective world. Shakespeare says in *Othello:* "Do deeds to make heaven weep, all earth amazed" [struck dumb with horror].

We are not projecting meanings; we are the Moses of the world soul's revelation of itself. Evolution has been leading to synthesis. It is the synthesis of the world and myself. All that is required on our part is an act of love. We no longer operate from an I-It position but from an I-Thou relationship to the world. Like God it is not wholly other but who we are in depth. It is not that all are the same but all are one: my spirit, the world spirit, the Holy Spirit. To deny the divine, by the way, is thus to diminish the dimensions of myself and my world. *How do I engage this moment as a provocateur of the world's energies?*

Nature has moral and aesthetic consciousness. The forces of nature faithfully and continually cooperate. The rain forests of Hawaii, for instance, are nurtured by minerals from the sands of the Gobi desert of China blown there by the winds. It is the hubris of human ego to think that only humankind has consciousness. An advantage of letting go of ego is finding the numinosity of the universe. Romantic poets were among the first to see the transcendental consciousness of nature, continually creative and animating all of us. The world is not only being created but creating. The universe is a creator in that it is continually engaged in producing more highly organized wholes. This zeal for unity without cancelling diversity is what is meant by evolution, the way creation happens. "Let there be light," did not simply happen but, like all revelations, is happening now. "Now" happens whenever ego gets out of the way long enough to let the light through.

God can mean the spaciousness of the Self, the ground of being — both human and natural, pure openness boundlessly expanding. We have personified God, and that can limit the mystery of transcendence by saying it does not transcend personhood. Paul Tillich said that God is not a person but is certainly no less than a person. Only the metaphor of spaciousness accommodates the transcendence that is absolute and limitless. What the Buddhists have called the void and what the best of science knows of the spaces in the universe is perhaps what we have also called God.

Transcendence has been a difficult concept for new age people to accept because of its association with dualism: God out there, we down here. But it is possible to understand God as transcendent and not dualistic. The divine is that which transcends individual limits *while including all that is.* Such power to combine polarities is the exceptional gift of the higher Self that cannot be divisive or divided. Transcendent is transcendent of divisions. Our fear of transcendence becomes groundless when the Everything is always and already within reach. To transcend is not to leave something behind but to gather it into a new synthesis. Transcendence is the opposite of exclusion. It preserves and elevates at the same time — precisely what we are attempting to do with our religion. Evolution is a series of transcendences.

When Yahweh says, "I am who I am," he means "I exist." The Self's first announcement to ego is that it exists. There is something archetypal in the human psyche that is a higher power than ego. Religion addresses that fact by offering a technology to approach it, that is, beliefs, morality, rituals, and devotion (personal love and loyalty to a God or saints). In addition, religious experience is a liberating moment of realization revealing how we are in touch with the ground of our own being. That moment feels like an intimate contact with the Ultimate and simultaneously with all of nature and with the depths of ourselves. In other words, it is a flash of an irrefragable and abiding unity of the human, the natural, and the divine. Religion *as an experience* does not have to be dualistic but can unite apparent polarities.

The realm of the transcendent is intrapsychic, not extrapsychic. The origin of religious experience and of God is the human psyche free of control by the ego. Origin means locus, not cause. Our experience of the divine is our experience of our own deepest reality. The unconscious is the depth the ego cannot plumb. The divine is the depth the ego cannot plumb. There is no self-standing, transcendent deity out there. "Immanence is the mode of God's transcendence," says Gregory Baum. There is no self-sufficient, omniscient, omnipotent intervener in human history by absolute creation or absolute redemption. God is not the wholly Other but the most inward reality of ourselves and nature. Mount Olympus is the human soul and all the universe.

Karl Rahner speaks of "the silent mystery that tastes like nothingness because it is infinity." The ground of being in the Buddhist perspective is that same pure spaciousness, void of concepts or of ego. This foundation of spaciousness in the psyche exactly mirrors the ground of the galaxies, also pure space. Any conscious spiritual view is a metaphor for a physical reality. All religions are natural religion in their origin. Every key belief in religion has a natural analogue from which it derives. For instance, resurrection has resonance in the rebirth of the earth in spring. Nature houses religious truths through the centuries like cathedrals, which are houses of God but can only be built of natural wood and stone.

The *anima mundi,* the soul of the world, *is* the cosmic unconscious. This is the Self that is simultaneously the soul of all the universe continually seeking incarnation in us and in all things. It is a center ever evolving and pulsing with life-producing energies. This is what is meant by God-creating. Spirits are not flying around out there but represent how archetypal energies want to incarnate in nature and in us. That passion of divinity for the human story is what is felt by us as being loved by God.

None of this cancels the existence of God but only relocates it. We are natively God-oriented. The experience of God and of the Self are identical. To say there is no God is not to find ourselves. A denial of God is a denial of our humanity and of all of nature since the psyche in both is geared toward the transcendent. The question is not whether God exists or how to prove it. The question is how the reality of the transcendent is manifesting itself in the world here and now through me and this and all of us.

The supernatural is the realm beyond conscious ego, the realm of limitlessness. We see it in dreams, in transcendent longings and actions, in synchronicities, in miraculous occurrences, in visions, intuitions, art, healings, prophetic realizations, conversions that accomplish what no amount of therapy can, and in myriad other ways. These supernatural means deserve our attention and our reverence since they are the pathways to the divine. The psyche is sacred because it is the *temenos* — sacred space — in which that human-divine encounter happens.

The Council of Chalcedon proclaimed the two natures of Christ, human and divine, in one person. This is a declaration about us. Our psychic maturation involves gradual realization of an unceasing continuity between human and divine. The unconscious, our deepest psychic reality, sponsors the journey to wholeness. Religion has the same purpose in human life. Within the human psyche is an irrepressible drive to live out its religious meanings. True religion facilitates the entry of these divine longings into the world of human feeling and action. This is how Chalcedon comes to be honored.

Catholicism — with all its flaws and failures — is unique among Christian religions for its long history of conserving the sacraments and rituals that enact the psyche's truths. A living Church is one that encourages access to inner divinity. This cannot happen when the body is held in contempt or when male clerics hold all the power. The work of the Church in the new millennium is to heal those divisions and to restore power to all the faithful. Just as God is not whole without the material, the feminine, or the shadow, neither is the Church.

A one-sided God and a one-sided devil result when we become caught up in dichotomies. Demons and deities happen because of our attachment to polarities rather than to harmony. Christ's suffering is a metaphor for the pain it takes to get to wholeness. The Cross symbolizes the opposites that are combined by hanging suspended between them and not dividing one against the other. To hold the opposites is to rise to a new united life, one in which there is amity, not enmity, in the psyche. Idolatry happens when one feature of the psyche assumes preeminence over all the others.

The champions of this unity were the mystics who proclaimed the infallible value of the inner life throughout the ages. The inner life referred to by mystics is the depth unconscious we know today. The mystics were discredited by the official Church. But the true Church has not always been the official Church. Its most harshly condemned heretics were often the saints keeping the heritage of faith alive. They were the martyr vestals keeping the flame of religious freedom alive until later generations could receive and bless the torch. Our suffering as we struggle with the official magisterium and the official precepts may be intense because we are not fighting our own battle only but that of our ancestors and heirs too. This is another dimension of the communion of saints. Golgotha is Adam's grave; Aeneas carries Anchises to safety; Christ harrows hell to apply his suffering to the liberation of the ancestors.

In Greek myth, Saturn eats his children. This is a metaphor for the inveterate proclivity of the old patriarchal guard to eat new ideas alive, to nip speculation and dreams in the bud. Perhaps this is to be expected as part of the human story. Religious authority gives us something to fight against and that helps us grow and establish our own beliefs. Niels Bohr said: "The opposite of a great truth is another greater truth."

The Divine Child: Archetype of Individuation

In the image of the Primordial Child, the world finds its own childhood, and everything that sunrise and the birth of a child mean for and say about the world. The childhood and orphan's fate of the child gods have not evolved from the stuff of human life but from cosmic life. What appears to be biographical in mythology is an anecdote from the world biography.... The child archetype represents the precious childhood aspect of the cosmic psyche. — CARL JUNG

There are similar stories surrounding the births of Buddha and Christ. Asita visited the newborn Buddha and wept that he would not live to see him as an adult. Simeon wept to hold Jesus in his arms and felt grateful to have lived long enough to see him. Perhaps many saints and ancestors came to our cradles to tell us how wonderful and important our births were. Perhaps our joy at a baby's birth is a realization that that child is a personification of the divine child archetype. The gifts of the Magi to Jesus mirrored his divinity. Gold, frankincense, and myrrh are gifts fit for a royal god. They are the gifts Christ gives back to us as we discover and acknowledge our affiliative identity. We want mirroring in our infancy because it is the necessary ingredient to development but also because the divine child archetype wants it too. The higher Self in us, the Divine Child, wants human mirroring. Every one of us wants and deserves a visit from the Magi.

The divine child motif in the hero story provides a striking symbol of the Self archetype and of the archetype of transformation. The divine child is the image of the divine that has come to be an assisting and effective resource in our battle with our ego fears and attachments. The divine child represents completed individuation. This archetype is not the inner child of psychology but the inner potential of the Self that wants to be born in us from the ashes of ego fear and clinging. The image of the helpless infant who is nonetheless a hero shows that our limitations and terrors enclose a hidden liveliness, a bud that wants to flower.

The divine child represents the hero archetype in its infancy. The hero is often an orphan who is unwelcome at birth. Examples are Moses, Jesus, Dionysus, and Horus. All these heroes were hidden after being born until it was safe for them to emerge and surprise the world with their true identity. They were cared for by women during this phase of their life. This is a metaphor for the times in our life when we have to be taken care of, be hidden away, lie low until the time is right, be nurtured by the anima, the soul. It is thus a time presided over by feminine, graceful energies rather than ego effort. The sense of the personal is feminine in this hour. Mary is the personification of the archetype of that character in our heroic journey. The riches in her are not found so easily when the accent is on proving her virginity as if it were meant to be taken literally. That trivializes the meaningfulness of the doctrine. It is about her and our direct access to the Source once there is no ego in the way. It is about the transpersonal possibilities behind appearances. Magical thinking and superstitious trust in her powers likewise make Mary an idol clutched by the untrusting ego that fears the dark side of the psyche and nature. We find Mary's warmest meaning when we let ourselves feel held in the dark by a maternal force of tenderness. That is a powerful and authentically consoling way to reclaim the riches Mary was always holding out to us in our religious past.

The divine infant is isolated but ultimately he joins everyone together. In his creative dimension, the divine child is the risk taker. In his dependency, he is the needy and endangered waif. He is vulnerable, and this is how eventually he empowers. These are the paradoxes that show us we have ventured into the spiritual world, the world where opposites unite, where no single appearance is enough, where the Everything is within reach. This is the world of Everest, at the summit of which one finds marine limestone. The top of the world was once the bottom of the sea.

The divine child is the Self, the wholeness that includes and expands consciousness, as a child includes his past genetic history and grows into his fuller future with time. The miraculous powers of the divine child and his resolute will to live symbolize our own psyche's vital urge toward individuation. The liveliness of a child is a perfect symbol for the yearning in us for self-realization, self-actualization, fulfillment of destiny, completion of life tasks, and contribution to the evolution of our species. The divine child thus represents the combination of all opposites. His miraculous powers and his painful bruises figure in the completion of humankind.

Here are the mythic characteristics of the divine child, recognizable from hero stories we know:

• His birth is miraculous, for example, virgin birth or dual birth: one parent is human; one is divine. This motif is psychic and metaphorical, not empirical or literal. It is about the ego-Self axis. We lose the power of an archetypal event when we take it literally. It can become magic when it represents only one unique historical event in which only one person is actualized. When it is appreciated as a metaphor, it gives us oracular information about the design, potential, and destiny of everyone's psyche. Since mythology was the first psychology, the hero stories were vehicles for an understanding of who we really are and what we were meant to become. The primal archetypal event is not limited then to one moment in time or to one special hero, but is happening at every moment in every one of us. There is only one story and it is ours.

• As darkness rises to protect itself, adversity befalls the divine child: "When one devil is expelled, seven more terrible than the first may appear," Jesus said. This is actually a good sign; evil is losing its grip and so it unleashes all its final troops against "something so powerful that, though newly born, it cannot be suppressed anymore," as Marie-Louise Von Franz says. That which is about to become extinct exaggerates itself just prior to extinction. But the miraculous birth wants to happen. We have the momentum of evolution on our side. Something more than ego strives for wholeness and will not be stopped.

• The infant is at once solitary and at home in the primeval world: "He came unto his own but his own received him not," writes St. John about Jesus. Few may welcome his birth, yet all are in need of it. Jesus was welcomed by the Magi and the shepherds but hated by Herod. Moses was hunted for death by the Pharaoh but welcomed by Pharaoh's sister. Horus was hidden in the papyrus swamp and cared for by Isis, who protected him from Set, the shadow god, who wanted to destroy him. Dionysus was disguised as a girl and guarded by Queen Ino when Hera sought his life.

• The ultimate triumph of the hero over the monster is a metaphor for the victory of consciousness over unconscious forces. Individuation requires a struggle. During the struggle, the hero — we Pinocchios — strike at the foe, strike out, fall into the void, are cared for by others, and are revived by a grace beyond our own making. We finally learn that the foe is within us and that friendship, not extinction, is the true goal of the work. This is why Jesus, Buddha, and the Dalai Lama are greater heroes than film idols who can kill the foe but cannot redeem him or reconcile with him and therefore never enrich themselves with his strengths. To kill off our religious past results in the same losses.

• The divine child is often abandoned by his friends at the beginning and end of his life. Since a child is always growing toward independence, detachment from his beginnings is necessary. Abandonment is a painful but sometimes necessary passage to this possibility. The abandoned child is the archetype of the part of us that is exposed and throws itself onto the mercy of the world. Such vulnerability is not victimization; it brings power with it. The willingness to take one's chances confers the power. This courage, like superior awareness, will feel like orphan aloneness throughout life. Yet higher consciousness is possible only in the context of this isolation and vulnerability.

• The paradox of the divine child is in his holding of two major opposites that plague us in life: vulnerability and power. To be stuck in fear is to be victimized by fear. We then do not hold both sides. Achilles is a personification of the courageous human ability to hold vulnerability and power simultaneously. His story acknowledges the wonderfully accommodating nature of the psyche and violates none of its multifarious qualities. Uniting opposites is the emblem of the child-hero as well as the central thrust of the work of befriending the dark side. Dorothy united the images of the simple farm hands and the heroic assisting forces of her journey through Oz. She thus endowed their lowliness with glory, adorning and transforming their weakness into strength. Dorothy accepted the conditions of Oz, that is, of her life at the time. This acceptance led to a daring spontaneity, just what it took to dissolve the witch's power and then to share it with her friends. She represents the divine child's power to participate in the flow of life consciously, no matter how beset with griefs, with no need to destroy it. *Can I embark on such a perilous enterprise?*

The Mandala: Rose Window of Individuation

A wisdom consciousness observing emptiness, which is a state arisen from meditation, is itself a meditative stabilization that is a union of calm abiding and special insight.... The main technique is for one consciousness to contain the two factors of observing a mandala circle of deities and simultaneously of realizing their emptiness of inherent existence. In this way, the vast, the appearance of deities, and the profound, the realization of suchness, are complete in one consciousness.

— DALAI LAMA, *Kindness, Clarity, and Insight*

It is useful to explore our theme from an Eastern perspective. The last sentence of the quotation above revisits a central point: the profoundest truths repose in every human heart. A mandala is a Buddhist picture of what all the words in the preceding pages have been saying. It is the good news about — or new awareness of — the psychological, spiritual, and mystical possibilities in ourselves. A mandala originates in the divine nucleus of the human psyche where such perfect wholeness always and already is.

A *mandala* is a four-sided figure, often containing a circle, used for meditation on the unity of Self and universe by Hindus and Buddhists. It is a spiritual cosmogram. Mandalas go back to Paleolithic times. In the eighth century, the mandala image was brought to Tibet from India by the great Buddhist teacher Padma Sambhava. It was meant to induce contemplation in a nondual way, by exposing the shape of the inner psyche in an external form. A mandala represents human longing for ultimate oneness and then makes it present. In Tibetan Buddhism, "mandala" also refers to a practice of teachings and rituals depicted in the circular design of the whole universe, including all the Bodhisattvas that assist us in our struggle with the demons of ego. Mandalas are offerings of the entire universe to Buddha, who will circle it and us with his compassion.

A mandala is a palace with four gates of entry in each of the four directions and a deity in the center. The mandala is a sacred blueprint and path to enlightenment. It is Buddha's heart, Christ's heart, our hearts. It is an ancient symbol of the continually unfolding mirror unity of the human soul and the wider universe. It depicts the reliable cooperation of the universe in our personal work. It displays the essential wholeness that we are and provides a road map for the existential journey toward our fulfillment. A mandala is a picture of the divine dimension-extension of human existence. It shows us that everything has a place in the world of spiritual wholeness. It is the tabernacle, the psychic palace, that grants equal housing to gods and worlds and us.

In Tibetan Buddhist art, a mandala is an externalization of the condition of wholeness, the center point of creative energy showing the phases of spiritual evolution. It is a chart of transpersonal unfolding. In it order and chaos coexist, and this is what makes it life-renewing. A mandala combines the opposites of conservation and creativity. According to Tibetan lore, a mandala protects our interior purposes from the clutches and seductions of demons, especially by reason of its roundness. The circle is the symbol of the Self. We hardly notice the many configurations of the mandala in the world around us: clock, compass, lotus, rose, face, labyrinth, diamond, flower, zodiac, square dances, halo, cathedral, rose window, pebble in a pond, flying saucers. A pendulum creates a mandala each day. A church is a mandala with the altar as the center and the doors as gates.

A mandala represents the ultimate unity of inner-outer and all apparent opposites. The ego cannot see a mandala. It can discern only a neat design. Only in the spiritual world is a mandala visible as itself. Then it shows us how everything is related, and we look at it as a whole, without partiality toward any single feature of it. A mandala is not a symbol of wholeness but a direct vision of it. It is a natural symbol removed from all conscious intention. Mandalas sometimes appear in dreams when wholeness is happening in us. The fact that the psyche spontaneously produces mandalas in dreams shows our inclination and ability to wrest order from disorder, our need for that order, and our containing of it. Mandalas reflect our transcendent longings and fulfillments.

The journey within a mandala is from the outer rim to the invisible center, the *bindu,* at once the center and pivot of the universe and of ourselves. The divine is the ground of this center. The center of the mandala is a paradoxical sacred point of meeting of all the planes of time and timelessness. The path to the center is through labyrinthine ways that represent the struggles along the heroic journey to wholeness, of which a mandala is the archetype. It is indeed the abode of the Self.

The center is eternal potential, the heart of all, the axis of the world. The concentric circles around the center are the phases of initiation and the evolving increases in consciousness. Contemplation of a mandala leads to change because it puts us in contact with the source of energy within ourselves since its center is our center. In fact, a mandala provides a centering technique. When we reach the center, we pivot out again to the world with the gifts of the Self. In the hero myth the arrival happens when we realize we were always and already at the goal. For nomads — and what else are we? — the center of the world keeps moving. The center of the mandala is anywhere we are when we wake up.

In Christian tradition, the mandala appears in St. Augustine's image of God as a circle, in the mystic Henry Suso's divine circle that is visible only to the "friends of God." The mandala is in the rose window of a cathedral and in the iconography of the four evangelists. Jung refers to the Renaissance theme of the Coronation of Mary as a mandala in that four figures appear: the Trinity and a human woman, surrounded by angels. (Notice also how, in this scene, heaven is incomplete without a human component, divinity is not complete without femininity.)

A quaternity is itself a symbol of wholeness. Thus there are four seasons in the complete year, four elements, four directions in nature. There are four functions in the psyche: thinking (represented by the sword suit in the Tarot), feeling (cup suit), sensation (pentacle suit), and intuition (wand suit). There are four cardinal virtues, four rivers of paradise, four gospels, and four horsemen of the Apocalypse. There are four cardinal signs in astrology, because of the seasons and elements that hinge on them: Aries (spring, fire), Cancer (summer, water), Libra (fall, air), and Capricorn (winter, earth).

Jung wrote: "A mandala is an attempt at self-healing on the part of nature, which does not spring from conscious reflection but from an instinctive impulse.... Mandalas lead us to the inner sacred precinct which is the source and goal of the psyche and contains the unity of life and consciousness." He also says that a mandala contains "the innermost god-like essence of man" and that "in modern mandalas the place of the deity is taken by the wholeness of man." An enlightened person is thus an embodiment of a mandala.

A mandala is an alchemical vessel in which our transformation is pictured and conjured. It is an expression of the self-integrating and self-healing reliable processes by which the psyche nurtures itself in time. It has the power to transmute daily life into an archetypal spiritual enterprise. It shows how daily life is always and already a locus of harmony and dynamism, like the universe itself. Jung refers to the mandala as a "cryptogram of the state of the Self presented anew each day." It is, in effect, the beatific vision of our wholeness, as Dante saw it in the form of a white rose in the last canto of *The Divine Comedy*.

> *As a practice, draw a mandala of your own life: begin with a flower with four petals in the shape of a cross. Place yourself in the center. In the upper petal, write or draw what is pressing on you and seems to be holding you back: afflicting forces. In the lower petal: place what is upholding and supporting you: assisting forces. In the right petal: what is trying to happen or to open for you. In the left petal: what has ended and needs to be let go of. (The right is east, the rising sun with new opportunity. The left is west, the setting sun with endings and grief.)*

> *The true mandala is an inner image gradually built through the active imagination when psychic equilibrium is disturbed or when a thought cannot be found and so must be sought for since it is not contained in any writing.*   — CARL JUNG

SEVEN

Familiar Pathways

The Cross

Most of us are familiar with the traditional Fall-Redemption paradigm of the Middle Ages. Matthew Fox has presented a model that more cogently describes how divine love works. The new emphasis in his creation theology has been on cosmic salvation and not simply on personal perfection. In the traditional view, revelation is something that happened as opposed to something that is happening. The old paradigm construes revelation as ending with the death of the last apostle. In this context, the work of the Church is to hold the revelation safe and intact. When revelation is construed as a happening, our challenge is to be more and more receptive to the ever renewed Word. "Revelation," said Gregory Baum, "is a happening and a happening is not a happening unless it is happening."

In the traditional view of redemption, it is accomplished once and for all by Jesus on the cross. He offered himself as the necessary ransom for the outrage of Adam's sin in the Garden of Eden. By virtue of baptism, we are sharers in the forgiveness that resulted from his death. This sharing of grace, however, does not remove the deep flaw that remains in us as a consequence of original sin. This is one of the main reasons that we are in need of conservator-father figures who alone have the special charism to rescue us from our ignorance. Left to ourselves, we might sully the integral deposit of faith or never find it. In the conservative perspective, we remain children that require paternal care. There is a direct relationship between many traditional beliefs and the patriarchal Church structure. One supports the other.

At the same time, we take notice of the archetypal wealth ever present in traditional beliefs: the need for purification is common in all religions. The ego is purified of its arrogance and ill will. Sprinkling water on the heads of the faithful was performed each afternoon in the temple of Isis at Pompeii in Christian times. The Nile was thought to be inhabited by Osiris and washing in it was a rite of purification. This is true even now of the Ganges. Water is universally associated with cleansing. Baptism is a cleansing and a drowning of ego so that it can be reborn in and as the Self. This is the core belief living in the accretions of centuries of dualism. A universal truth underlies the sacrament of baptism. Every faith belief and ritual has just such a core.

In traditional view, death, suffering, and the other givens of existence, are the wages of sin. The redemption theology begins with sin. In the new paradigm, the life energy of the universe is also our life energy. This energy is displayed and nurtured by the givens of existence and our response to them. In this context, suffering is part of how life evolves and death is how life transits to a new mode of being.

In the traditional redemption theology, there is little emphasis on the cosmic Christ-Self who loves the human-divine milieu, where humans err and then are transformed. In the old view, human beings are sinners, not powerful stewards of the universe. Our eternal life comes after death, after suffering, after falling and being forgiven. Is there room in our hearts for the wonderful news that eternal life is happening here and now? The cross is a significant fact of any human journey, but so is the new life of Resurrection and Pentecost, in both of which we are invited to co-create a new world.

Sinners who are weighed down by guilt are not usually oriented toward co-creating. The ascetic life then may take precedence over an attitude of joy. Mortification brings dualism into the spiritual life. The healthy alternative is a commitment to self-discipline in the fulfillment of a goal. Underlying the fall-redemption approach is a suspicion about and an impugning of the human body. "The soul makes war on the body," St. Augustine says. Meister Eckhart, on the other hand, believes that the soul loves the body. (These two traditions have always existed in the Church, but in our childhood we knew only the life-denying one. In our present adult life we are hearing the other side, and it matches what we always carried deep within our psyches as the truth.)

Implicit in the dualistic view is the search for holiness with a Jesus-and-I separatist flavor. What a sharp contrast to this more contemporary theological understanding expressed by Matthew Fox: "Holiness is cosmic hospitality." He is actually reflecting St. Thomas's description of our spirituality as a "connectedness with all things." This is the meaning of mysticism: connection and communion: people and nature, people and people, people and God. (In this context, access to God does not require the mediation of patriarchal authority.) Bruno

Borchert, in his book *Mysticism: Its History and Challenge,* says that this mystical tradition is universal and though it may differ externally, "in essence it is everywhere the same: it is the experimental knowledge that, in one way or another, everything is interconnected, that all things have a single source."

Rituals

Rituals acknowledge, enact, and establish the triune ratio of the natural, the divine, and the human: they join the things of nature with human words and gestures in honor of the transcendent life. Rituals create the consciousness they represent. We can come to them without full faith and find more faith engendered by our participation in them. We bring our own givens, our own beliefs, and rituals supply and support us in our move toward wholeness. Regarding rituals, Bernard Cooke says in *Sacrament and Sacramentality:*

> A religious view looks for the meaning of everyday reality by looking beyond what is given to a more all-encompassing reality. Through ritual a total person is engulfed and transported into another mode of existence. In ritual the world as lived and the world as imagined fuse, thereby providing a transformation in one's sense of reality. Thus it is out of the context of concrete acts of religious observance that religious convictions emerge.
>
> Ritual is the means for providing the conviction that religious concepts are true; it also makes the culture's ethos reasonable and makes sense of unwelcome contradictions in life. Rituals are symbolic actions expressive of the community's symbolic narratives or sacred stories. These expressions move toward interpreting and understanding the meaning and nature of life, and within our rituals the common life of the community is acted out in the context of remembering, "re-presenting," and anticipating its memory and vision. Our rites are at the center of human life, binding past, present, and future together. Without meaningful and purposeful rituals daily life cannot be made or kept fully human.

In the Diamond Sutra, Buddha compares the teachings, rituals, and images of faith to a raft that is used to get us to the other side of our faith journey. Once we have arrived at a sincere adult consciousness of spirituality and religion, we leave the raft behind and continue our journey on foot. To carry the raft with us would slow us down. A spiritual consciousness includes this sense of the temporariness and the disposability of the means that lead us to the end. St. Thomas, in one of his hymns to the Eucharist, looks to the time when earthly images and mortal forms will yield to the awesome reality beyond forms. Then the veil over the tabernacle falls and we are with Jacob in the House of God at the Gate of Heaven. This is the same idea.

Religion includes rituals that celebrate passages along the journey of life. All the rituals and practices of religion are means of accessing love, wisdom, and healing. This is how they are valuable. "Sacrament" is derived from the Latin word for *mysterion,* a Greek word that means initiation. Every human passage to higher consciousness is an initiation into the world beyond ego. Initiation is an encounter with the conditions of existence and a rite of passage through them. They do not yield; we do.

Prayer is attention to this divine life of the Self. The sacraments of the Church happen at milestones on our human journey. They are celebrations of passages that are powerful and transformative. In this sense, they produce what they signify. They happen in community, like all passages, and so are witnessed by others. Some of our young people have turned to ancient styles of initiation such as piercing and tattooing. When our archetypal longings are not adequately addressed by our sacraments, it becomes harder for people to appreciate the riches of our religious rituals. Our challenge is to renew and reconstruct our sacraments to make them relevant in ways that have broad appeal.

Sacraments mediate an experience of the divine to us but cannot take the place of what they mediate. Sacraments, dogmas, creeds, rituals: all mediate the revelation of the human unconscious. Sacraments show the grace-bearing power of nature: bread, wine, oil, incense, fire, water, wax. It is ironic that throughout so much of its history, the Church used the forces of nature to kill free thought: for example, fire and oil to burn witches and heretics, water to drown or test them.

As we grow up in faith we realize that sacraments do not have to be limited to traditional forms since divine life infinitely disperses itself in unlimited ways. As adults with spiritual consciousness we can use the things of nature to design more means of grace than the seven the Church offers. In fact, the tradition of sacramentals has always encouraged us to do this. Sacramentals are things and rituals that help us find grace. The heroic journey archetype includes sacramentals in the form of altars, amulets, and talismans. Catholicism has maintained these in its tradition. Altars are associated with Mass, but we can create our own altars at home or in our gardens. An altar is then a personal shrine that honors what is meaningful in our life, a place of stability and refuge in daily conflicts. An amulet is a medal with an inscription that we wear to maintain a sense of accompaniment by assisting spiritual forces. It reminds us that we are not alone in the world of ego but partake in a kingdom beyond it. An amulet draws the forces of the cosmos to its wearer, who becomes the center of them. This sense of centeredness is what establishes our connectedness. A talisman is an active and transforming object that gives a sense of protection. A rosary is an example.

We can create our own sacramentals and discover means of grace in nature. The creative challenge to us is to design altars, talismans, and amulets, with natural objects, exalted and lowly. Huston Smith suggests we "think of the links of the great Chain [of Being] as gradations in degree to which matter hosts Spirit and becomes translucent to it." In addition, we can carry or honor cherished family heirlooms such as jewelry that have spiritual resonance for us. This is a way of having recourse to the communion of saints, our ancestors in the faith. None of this has to become magic, but any of it can be miraculous.

The Self configures itself differently in each unique personality. We each carry a different image of the divine, just as icons depict Christ differently, yet Christ is the same. We each have our unique ways of contacting the numinous. Brother Lawrence found God in the clutter of the kitchen; Moses found God in a cloud. Anything we experience can grip us with divine fervor. This is why religion cannot be narrow or sacraments limited. To be transformed by any numinous experience is a religious conversion. Any depth experience is religious experience and sacramental. This includes dreams, synchronicity, predicaments, symptoms, crises, relationships, heroics, the void, visions, responses to nature, and any other experience that grips us with a force that outstrips the ego's powers. To work through our life conundrums is as much an experience of grace as making a confession.

Nature is meant to be part of healing in therapy and a means of grace in religion. This must be how astrology, crystals, plants, and totem animals, became so important in the evolution of religion. What herbs are to medicine, nature is to religion. St. Francis is the exemplar of the truly religious man since he found the divine in matter. The mystery of the Incarnation is that God needs a tabernacle which is time long and space wide, and only we humans are limited enough to become it.

Patriarchal religion devalued human rhythms: the material, the feminine, the body, and nature. Religious teachings have often used misleading metaphors, ones that do not resonate with these cadences of the psyche. Catholics want the freedom to make faith relevant and not to see adaptations that honor experience discounted. We need a faith that critiques us but also invites us to leap. That is how it is transcendent after all.

> *What men took for truth stares one everywhere in the eye and begs for sympathy.* — HENRY ADAMS at Chartres

Prayer

Prayer has bad press among the humanists. It seems to betoken dualism, an address to a God-out-there. It is also suspect when it seems to serve the ego by petitioning for fulfillments of desires and maintenance of attachments. It can seem superstitious and magical when it asks for a repeal of the conditions of existence. Then it is the ego's entitlement at work. How can we appreciate prayer as a sincere and useful tool for spirituality?

It is now clear that religion is a built-in feature, enduring and necessary, of the human psyche. This interior function expresses itself through beliefs, moral behavior, rituals, and devotion. These four practices are some of the means by which the personal ego can discover its transpersonal purposes. Prayer is the dialogue or soliloquy that emerges from the relationship between the ego and the higher Self. It is not something to be afraid of or to be looked down on. It is a creative way to articulate the incarnation of divinity in our homespun life. Prayer can take many directions. Three words help us find our direction: yes, please, and thanks. These are the prayers of assent, intention, and thanksgiving.

The unconditional yes to the conditions of existence is the prayer of *assent*. We pray this way when we accept the reality of our life predicament and honor it as a path. Something happens that we cannot fix or change or stop. We acknowledge ourselves as facing destiny, and we surrender to its stern reality. That is the prayer of assent and, like all prayer, it requires no words. It is simply a reverence for reality itself as a transpersonal will with a meaning yet to be revealed. Examples of this prayer in words are: "I accept the things that cannot change." "I say yes to my here and now situation and to all that will come of it." "I let go of having to understand this and let it be."

When we want something to happen for ourselves or others, we can place a firm *intention* for it. It is a spiritual enterprise when it has unconditional love, perennial wisdom, and healing power as its purpose. It is ego-driven — and therefore not prayer — when it has self-aggrandizement, greed, or vindictiveness as its purpose. Here are examples of the prayer of intention: "I change the things that can be changed." "May I have the wisdom to know the difference between what can and cannot be changed." "May I become more loving toward those I dislike." "May all beings benefit from my spiritual practices."

The prayer of *thanksgiving* is an acknowledgment of the powers of the higher Self. It is a form of praise and appreciation for the gifts of grace. This sense of gratitude is prayer. It can be expressed verbally as: "For all that has been: thanks." "I am thankful for all I have and for all I can give." "I am thankful for all the good things that have resulted from my life sufferings and crises."

All three directions of prayer can be expressed by affirmations, verbally or silently. They also can be forms of meditation. Mindfulness meditation is a powerful way to sit in the center of all three directions of prayer. By sitting and paying attention to our breathing we let go of the ego's chatter of fear and desire. We become fair and alert witnesses of the passing show of our existence. A shift occurs from identifying with what happens and simply attending to it. We thereby say yes to the reality of ourselves as liberated from the dualism that ego is so adept at creating. We relate to our experience rather than being possessed by it. We enter the silent gap between our struggles and let go of judgment, fear, desire, the need to fix or control, and attachment to an outcome. In this silent spaciousness, our true Self, a clarity and serenity can open. Then it is easier to say yes and please and thanks. Such mindfulness in daily life situations fulfills St. Paul's suggestion that we "pray always."

Here are some prayerful declarations of spiritual wholeness that show the use of affirmations:

- I am always opening myself to more consciousness, that is, more light. I notice what I am up to, what my agenda is, where my potential is.

- Sometimes I fall down in my resolve to love generously. I admit this without despair. I accept myself as I am, neither condoning all I have done nor castigating myself. I make amends to those I have hurt. I accept responsibility for the consequences of all I have caused.

- I create an atmosphere of forgiveness and mendable failures in all my relationships. No one is perfect and no one is permanently excluded from my circle of love. I am never at ease as long as I have even one grudge.

- I see that the armor that was protecting me from fear was actually preventing me from being fully free of it. I admit my fears, feel them fully, act as if they were not able to stop me, and find an alternative that frees me from them. With this program, I am combining defenselessness and resourcefulness.

- I see that acknowledging a higher power does not excuse me from even one of the conditions of ordinary existence but may grant me more resilience, optimism, and resources in facing them. I acknowledge that spirituality is like an immune system: it does not prevent sickness but it does make for faster recovery and sometimes less susceptibility.

- I trust that I have a unique destiny. Everything that happens is part of its unfolding. Synchronous events and meetings keep happening for just that reason. It is for that same reason that I was given this lifetime. Everything is perfect.

- My destiny is to reach mystical union through a healthy personality and an evolved spirituality. My destiny is thus a holy communion of the human, the natural, and the divine. I make a fervent commitment to love wisely and to shower healing upon my world. Many invisible technologies aid me in this.

- Grace is the life force that energizes my spiritual potential. This force is the same in me, in nature, and in God.

The Eucharist

The Eucharist is the living archetype of spiritual nurturance, "the true Bread that has come down from heaven." Bread is earthly and finite. Something mortal becomes immortal sustenance. This is a way of referring to our own identity and our own destiny, earthbound and yet having a transearthly origin and end. Bread and wine are fruits of nature. The natural is to the human as it is to the divine. The Eucharist is a uniquely powerful and touching way to articulate the triune ratio. The Eucharist is also the archetype of the Self as that which continually nourishes the ego on its faith journey. All we have is not enough; something greater than any identity we can name is always at work serving a supper to the soul.

In religions the world over, sacred rituals present a transition: at first the devotee acknowledges and adores the god. That reverence is meant as a preparation for the climactic gift-event of becoming one with the god in communion. From ancient times, to consume was to assume the identity of the deity. The Christian Eucharist is the meal of the believing community, which sustains and develops it. From the alchemical point of view, it is the greatest representation of the mystery of transformation: the least valued nutritionless thing is really the most valuable, all-nourishing thing. This reverse of the ordinary is visible only to those who have learned to see in a new way: what to anyone else is worthless is, to someone who has been initiated, the most cherished of all realities. The Eucharist is the way the ego can transcend itself and enter the world of the Self.

There is a touching intimacy in the Eucharist since the granting of it and the good-bye of Jesus happened at the same supper. The Eucharist is the way Jesus found to stay with us. Why else does he give it to us on his last night on earth? It is the supremely sensitive gift of a "tremendous lover" of humankind. He knew what it meant to feel bereft, and he addressed and healed that in the gift of his ongoing presence in the Eucharist. Presence in a sustaining way is the deepest meaning of compassion. Compassion is accompaniment. St. Augustine says, in a sermon on the Eucharist: "The body of Christ gives the body of Christ to the body of Christ." The presence is in all of us in all our uniquely diverse ways. The Real Presence in the Eucharist refers to an access to God through the host. Since the deepest reality of human beings is divine, anytime someone is really present to us, we are in the presence of a Blessed Sacrament, a living corporeal epiphany of divinity.

The Eucharist indeed shows the transparence of all matter: something behind appearances is personal and loves us. Bread becomes the power that captures and mediates the love in the universe, that which moves and motivates evolution. The Mass speaks directly to the impermanence of the world since it is always anchoring us. It is *this*, the same no matter what is happening in the changing tides. Jung saw the Mass as the supreme rite of individuation since it has to do with the finding of human wholeness. The Mass does not repeat a past event but reveals an ever living event: a mystery beyond the capacity of ego to comprehend since in it opposites unite. It is not a repetition of the Last Supper but a renewal of its promise of divine life in us. What is that life? It is love of all people and nature, respect for inner wisdom, and ongoing incarnation in the world of our evolving spiritual consciousness. "Inner," after all, also means within a human bond, the realm between humans.

The Mass is a community event that provides an emblem for the divine life become really present in us, for us, and with us. It is the archetype of nourishment, the viaticum on the journey to individuation and spiritual wholeness. It is to be eaten as a life-giving food, an assisting force of strength-giving power on our path. In it Christ is present as an intimate partner and so it is a form of union. All the metaphors of Christianity apply to other traditions too. The Eucharist is unique because it is about Jesus only. It is a special connection to him and a way of accessing his gifts and his Spirit. To cherish it and become it is our Christian destiny.

The Mass is the most elegant and deeply religious rite ever devised. It has endured because it combines the four elements of religion (belief, morality, ritual, and devotion) with the three elements of the divine Self (love, wisdom, healing) in the context of the triune equation (nature, divinity, and humanity).

> *From the moment that you said "This is my Body" not only the bread on the altar, but to a certain extent everything in the universe became yours and nourishes in our souls the life of grace and the spirit.... The Holy Eucharist is in fact extended throughout the universe and so constitutes a promise of its eventual transfiguration.... It captures all the power of loving in the universe and extends beyond the Host to the cosmos itself, which the still unfinished Incarnation gradually transforms in the course of the passing centuries.... From the beginning a single event has been developing in the world: the Incarnation, realized in each individual through the Eucharist.... All the communions of all men, present, past, and future, are one communion.... Right from the hands that knead the dough to the hands that consecrate it, only one Host is being formed by the totality of the world and all the duration of time is needed for its consecration.... This is a truly universal transubstantiation in which the words of consecration fall not only upon the sacrificial bread and wine, but also on the totality of joys and sorrows occasioned in the course of evolution.... In the Host, it is my life you are offering me, O Jesus.*
> — PIERRE TEILHARD DE CHARDIN

The Sacred Heart

The best image of God's nature is that of tender care that will not be lost. — ALFRED NORTH WHITEHEAD

The image of Christ's heart is an externalizing of the unconditional love of God in us. It reflects our own deepest identity. The heart of Jesus with its unending and all-embracing love is the template of every human heart. That image of divine actuality reflects our human potentiality. We already have the love that can free us from ego fear. It is just a matter of noticing it, of seeing it, of showing it. As we let go of ego (a painful, scary process) we radiate the love that makes our hearts like that of Jesus: open, vulnerable, giving.

The Sacred Heart has a longstanding devotion in the Church. It was made popular in recent centuries because of the visions of St. Margaret Mary. In the context of her time, the promises of the Sacred Heart made sense. Today the ones that are not biblically rooted may seem superstitious. An adult in faith can distinguish the divine origin of a vision from subjective elements in the visionary: personality, historical context, influences on the visionary. All these affect the content of the message that has to be rethought for today's world.

The Sacred Heart is a living symbol. In a symbol, a reality presents itself. A symbol is another Real Presence. A sign and what it signifies are separate. A symbol is distinct but not separate. A symbol can change into a sign, for example, a class ring on a boy who was expelled. The human body is a symbol of the human person, the self-presentation of the soul. The body is the bodiliness of a spiritual presence. "The highest knowledge of spirit is corporeal," said Karl Rahner. All beings are thus symbolic because they have to express themselves to be themselves, precisely the nature of a symbol. Symbols proclaim, reveal, express, and concretize reality. For instance, the soul animates the body and makes it real in time and space.

The Incarnation affirms that all human beings have the capacity for divinization. Faith actualizes this potency. The Church is a symbol of the human life of Jesus.

The sacraments are the symbols of the central sacrament: the Church. True devotion happens when we see Christ's heart as the mirror of and call to our own destiny of love. The heart is the core of our lively energy and wholeness. Jesus' heart affirms the deepest core of the universe and of God. It is the symbol of an unconditional gift of himself that Jesus makes to us. The supreme Self of all the universe and time thus enters the bodymind of our limitations. The heart is the point of meeting of Self and matter. "The tangible existence of a human person can itself be a symbol and a sacrament," said Martin Buber.

The heart of Jesus is the reality of the convergence of opposites that characterize the spiritual journey. The pierced heart entirely open, always giving, fully committed, unfailingly loving whether or not we love in return: "Since Christ does not release us from his fate, let us hope that we will discover in our association with the sacrament of his heart what we will be and what we really are," wrote Karl Rahner.

The central point of the devotion to the Sacred Heart is challenge and capacity, not promises. It is a call to love of others. Once we say that God is not one being among others, we can only love God by loving others. The urgency to elicit from our hearts the fullness of its love is the essence of the devotion to the Sacred Heart. In fact, devotion empowers us to do it. An adult devotion to the heart of Jesus free of superstition is yet to appear in the Church. That is a true loss to the passionate spirituality of devotion, an essential feature of the religious instinct. Every one of us can contribute to new paradigms that enliven and renew something that so touchingly represents the integration of personal love and spiritual evolution.

The revelations of the Sacred Heart in the seventeenth century to St. Margaret Mary are a turning point in the history of our understanding of the nature of the divine. This was the first time God showed a need, a longing for love from human beings. This is a great compliment to us and our capacity for love. In spiritual maturity, longing is dangerous if we become attached to it. The mystery of the Sacred Heart shows that divinity *includes* longing, as was evident at the Last Supper: "Long have I longed to eat this passover with you before I suffer." This longing of God for human beings is a metaphor for how the Self needs the ego to incarnate its light into the world. Divine life is not free-floating or external but relies on people and all of nature to make its presence felt. The message of the heart of Jesus is not superstitious promises but an awareness of the connection of the human and the divine.

The Sacred Heart is the supreme image of the heart of the Self, our limitless potential to love. There are many striking images that appear in human imagination and in dreams that depict its grandeur. Here is a reworking of the traditional litany of the Sacred Heart using these images:

> Heart of Jesus, in whom there is only yes, alive in me for the good of all humankind.
>
> Heart of Jesus, through the heart of Mary, alive in me for the good of all humankind.
>
> Heart of Jesus, center of my heart, alive in me for the good of all humankind.
>
> Heart of Jesus, gate of Paradise, alive in me for the good of all humankind.

Heart of Jesus, aglow with divine love, alive in me for the good of all humankind.

Heart of Jesus, worthy of unending honor, alive in me for the good of all humankind.

Heart of Jesus, replete with all the treasures of wisdom and knowledge, alive in me for the good of all humankind.

Heart of Jesus, from whose fullness we are all receiving, alive in me for the good of all humankind.

Heart of Jesus, desire of the everlasting hills, alive in me for the good of all humankind.

Heart of Jesus, life force of nature and the universe, alive in me for the good of all humankind.

Heart of Jesus, patient and most merciful, alive in me for the good of all humankind.

Heart of Jesus, bountiful to all who turn to you, alive in me for the good of all humankind.

Heart of Jesus, fountain of grace and holiness, alive in me for the good of all humankind.

Heart of Jesus, loving intent behind every twist of fate, alive in me for the good of all humankind.

Heart of Jesus, pierced to open, never to close, alive in me for the good of all humankind.

Heart of Jesus, source of all consolation, alive in me for the good of all humankind.

Heart of Jesus, my life, my death, and my resurrection, alive in me for the good of all humankind.

Heart of Jesus, pledge of eternal tenderness, alive in me for the good of all humankind

Heart of Jesus, center and joy of nature, alive in me for the good of all humankind.

Heart of Jesus, harmony of all universes, alive in me for the good of all humankind.

Heart of Jesus, consumed with compassion, alive in me for the good of all humankind.

Heart of Jesus, freedom from fear and grasping, alive in me for the good of all humankind.

Heart of Jesus, freedom for generosity and healing, alive in me for the good of all humankind.

Heart of Jesus, design and destiny of every earthly love, live in me for the evolution of all people and things.

Mary

When the time had come for God to realize his Incarnation, he had to raise up in the world a virtue capable of drawing him as far as ourselves.... He created the Virgin Mary, that is to say, he called forth on earth a purity so great that, within this transparency, he would concentrate himself to the point of appearing as a child. There, expressed in its strength and reality, is the power of purity to bring the divine to birth among us.

— PIERRE TEILHARD DE CHARDIN

In the fourth century A.D., the mystery religions were popular in the Roman world. The Great Mother was the central deity. The worship of the Great Mother was tied to nature worship; places in nature were sacred to her: springs, grottoes, hillsides, moon and stars. The cult of Mary arose in that context, though not simply in imitation of it.

The Great Mother was worshiped on this planet from the beginning. When her shrines were laid waste, nature continued her own hymn of praise. In early Christian times, there was a saying: "Forsaken Eleusis celebrates herself." Mary, in Christian times, supplanted Isis and Demeter as the archetypal figure of the Great Mother. All the pagan elements of goddesses were transferred to a new object. This is not idolatry since the psyche always knew that nature is feminine and deserves respect. Nature is trusted as a mother who renews our life even when all else is passing. May was chosen as Mary's month because it is a time of renewal, a recognition that the return of new life is reliable. We are part of nature and live in those same cycles. Every one of us is meant to be what Mary is.

In the Middle Ages, God was understood in theology as pure act and could not include a receptive side. There was also an accent on justice as requiring retribution. The psyche cannot be fooled; it always knew these were male-constructed limited ego perspectives. The image of Mary worked to provide what was missing in the full archetype of divinity. The Holy Spirit was originally honored as feminine, but later the Holy Spirit too was masculinized.

St. Anselm wrote: "God is the father of all created things and Mary is mother of all re-created things." Devotion to the Mother of God became devotion to God the mother. These were not theological distortions as much as archetypal recognitions. The male image of God is not sufficient and cannot satisfy the manifold longings of the human psyche. Some compensation is necessary in a masculine-ideal religion like Catholicism. It comes in the form of Mary but also in Eastern and alchemical perspectives. All these put the emphasis in spiritual work on drawing out what is within, not nailing in to us that which comes from without.

To ascribe female attributes to a male God misses the point. One figure cannot accommodate all that, as the trinitarian deity in so many religions shows. Mary is a necessary character in the full cast of divinity. The primordial knowledge of polytheism was taken literally and was unsophisticated, but the concept behind it is a solid one: divinity is a spectrum with all the archetypal possibilities in it: mother, father, divine child, hero, shadow, trickster, wise and compassionate guides, tempters and temptresses. It is not that there are many gods but that our human-divine nature and goal is polyvalent, that is, many powered. The task of faith is not to reassign the qualities of Mary to God but to preserve her unique place in our faith experience. Feminine energy is not a supplement to masculine energy. It is its complement.

Mary is not a symbol of God's feminine side or even a personification of it: she is another figure in the pantheon required for beings as diverse and complex as ourselves. Neither male nor female divinities alone have satisfied the human soul; both are necessary. It is not that a male God is just and Mary is forgiving and will hold back his wrath. The creative and the destructive and every set of opposites coexist in the full panoply of divinity. (Destructive means dissolving of ego.) All are necessary and work in a harmonious axis. There is justice and mercy and advocacy in the divine masculine as well as in the divine feminine.

Today there is less accent on Mary in the Church, and this represents both a gain and a loss. It is a gain when liturgy takes precedence over devotionalism. But Mary brings a necessary element to the life of faith: she represents the alchemical vessel that gestates and brings forth the Source and Redeemer of life.

Jung referred to the Annunciation, the visit of the angel Gabriel to Mary, as a perfect metaphor for how the archetypal world breaks in upon our transitory universe. The angelic and the human, the male and the female, the infinite and the finite meet in that moment. This is another powerful metaphor for our own destiny to reconcile opposites and gain entry through time to the world beyond time. We acknowledge the presence of the transcendent in our little room and we become filled with it so that we can deliver it to the world we love as Mary did once and still does.

Unfortunately, Mary is an injured archetype. What has been handed down to us in the images of Jesus and Mary lacks wholeness. It is up to us to expand the images with the full powers they deserve. Mary needs to be filled out with other qualities of the female, not only motherliness and receptivity but passion, friendliness, the power to renew, and intimacy. She is an inadequate archetype when she is all-giving and all-nurturing with no limiting darker side. A childish need to have a mother who is only kind and never limit-setting is reflected in the traditional archetype of Mary. It is a challenge to adult faith to find the dissolving power of our Mother, to ask her to dismantle our ego. In all cultures and times, the female was the archetype of the dissolution of the male ego. The patriarchal Church certainly needs the full experience of Mary. The archetype of the Mother of God is thus also a vehicle to describe how the divine becomes conscious, that is, by female energy, by nurturant love, by motherly care. Mary is the archetype of the psyche itself, for it truly gives birth to God. In this sense, Mary is ourselves when the incarnation-individuation process has happened to us. She is the model of our destiny to bring to birth the divine in the human.

Mary's human life is the fullness of grace. The dogmas of the immaculate conception of Mary and her assumption bodily into heaven do not simply delineate privileges. They tell us when she was first special and whether it ever changed. She is the exemplar of all us humans: we are radically acceptable, graced from the beginning by the graciousness of divine love. Paul Tillich spoke of God as the ground of being but he defines it this way: "the mother quality of giving birth, carrying, and embracing, and, at the same time, of calling back, resisting independence of the created, and swallowing it." He sees both sides of the eternal Self in God. Both sides of the eternal Self are in Mary too.

Karl Rahner says that in each epoch of history the image of Mary revealed the culture's expectation of women. In the early Church, she was the model of asceticism and restraint. In medieval times, she represented courtly love and was called the Queen of Heaven. In the nineteenth and twentieth centuries, she became the stainless ideal of harmony as a refuge from this wounded world. Yet in all times, Mary reveals the warmth in the divine life in us, our nurturant station at the heart of life.

O Holy Blessed Lady, constant comfort to humankind, your compassion nourishes us all. You care about those in trouble as a loving mother for her children. You are there when we call, stretching out your hand to push aside anything that might harm us. You even untangle the web of fate in which we may be caught, even stopping the stars for us if they form a pattern in any way harmful. — APULEIUS TO ISIS

> *Divinest patroness, and midwife gentle*
> *To those that cry by night, convey thy deity*
> *Aboard our dancing boat....*
>
> SHAKESPEARE, *Pericles*

EIGHT

Fifteen Ways Faith Grows Up

This chapter summarizes and expands the ideas in the preceding chapters.

1. Full Life over Limited Mind

The main characteristic of adult faith is that it has more to do with living than with intellectual postulation. Constructs help us organize our sense of reality. They work for us only when they are perceived as abstractions that help us conceptualize. I may say, "I believe that the president is doing a good job." This is a statement based on an intellectual assessment of the facts as I interpret them. It does not become real until I vote for his reelection. A belief is thus an ineffective, impotent thought until it translates itself into a congruent action that demonstrates a commitment. This happens by faith in action, faithwork, the works of mercy. It also happens by individuation, our personal work on ourselves to let our ego serve the purposes of the Self.

If I say I believe in the Resurrection, for example, but do not shape my life in accord with that belief — translate it into personal and other-directed action — it exists solely in my mind. I am giving what Cardinal Newman called "notional assent" instead of "real assent." Adult faith means real assent, that is, what is internally held is externally manifested. For example, to shape my life in accord with belief in the Resurrection means first of all that I am personally free from fear. Notice in the post-Resurrection appearance stories in the Gospels the repeated phrase: "Be not afraid." Before the Resurrection St. Peter feared a powerless serving-girl. After it, he defied authorities that had the power to kill him. Here are statements of a committed faith in the Resurrection that demonstrate its effects in daily life and its connection to human wholeness. This is the culmination of faithwork:

To say that Jesus is alive is to affirm:
I have nothing left to fear and I act that way even when I feel
fear.
I am detached from worldly gain and act that way.
I am free from fearful obsessions about death and act that way.
My life has a worth that does not have to be earned.
I know something about my destiny that makes me joyous in
good times and helps me handle tough times effectively and
optimistically.
I share this news not by persuading or proving but by word and
deed.
I have changed and keep changing.

These statements provide examples of how an internal belief becomes external, that is, complete and integrated. To have faith in an adult way is to create this kind of congruence between every belief and behavior. This means there is no longer a dichotomy between personal psychological work and spiritual practice. It is all one experience of individuation that honors our human-divine nature. There is no longer a dichotomy between ourselves and nature. There is no longer a difference between loving ourselves and loving others. Adult faith is a faith of equations, not divisions.

As we grow up in faith, we put less accent on individualistic salvation ("Jesus and I") and more accent on redeeming the planet. We see ourselves as part of a mystical body, the human community, and we care enormously about its fate and history. Faith becomes truly mature in the same way that relationships become mature: we see beyond our own narcissistic needs and offer someone beyond ourselves our love and attention. Social, political, and ecological consciousness joined with action characterize adult believers. They have transcended narrow personal limits and now love limitlessly. "Politics and the life of the spirit are inseparable," Gandhi said. Values for an adult are consistently applied to social concerns. There are no single-issue politics in a life of moral integrity. If I cherish the value of a human life, I may oppose abortion as a personal choice, but then I also oppose war-making and capital punishment. I am still consistent if I oppose abortion personally but am in favor of the availability of safe abortions to those who choose them. This is because I value freedom and because my values are personal and not to be imposed on others. Otherwise, I become an external authority dictating to others, and the vicious cycle of abuse of liberty continues.

As we grow up in faith we integrate community beliefs with personal questing. The story of the Holy Grail, one of the greatest myths of our Western tradition, demonstrates this. Why seek the chalice of the Eucharist when it is accessible at every Mass every day? Because it is not enough only to participate in the community's historical rituals. One must also move out on one's own: "enter the forest where there is no path." Our life of faith as a heroic journey is both communal and personal. We tread the path already trod by our ancestors in faith, and we blaze our own path. We are followers *and* pioneers. The greatest challenge of adult faith is to take a journey outside the ordinary, outside the tried and true, to our own unique configuration of the mystery into which we will be initiated. The second greatest challenge is to honor our faith inheritance at the same time.

2. Freedom from Fundamentalism

The appearance of extreme fundamentalism in the Americas becomes understandable once we realize that opposites constellate automatically in the psychic world. The rampant secularization of the past fifty years had to produce a pendulum reaction: right-wing fundamentalism. This is the ultimate danger of desacralization. We cannot get away with being irreligious. Human beings require religious consciousness, and when it is not honored, its hyperbole will arise in repressive and anti-pluralist ways. Opposites constellate in the psychic life of people and nations. The thesis of "no value in religion" that began in earnest in the 1960s led directly to the antithesis of widespread right-wing Christian fundamentalism. Today liberals are paying the price of our abandonment of religion as we see the nonpluralistic right gain ascendancy in politics. To throw the baby out with the bath water is to open the floodgates of religious puerility and bigotry. Reclaiming the riches of our religion may lead to the synthesis that waits to follow the extremes.

A grown-up in faith will not be a fundamentalist, one who takes things literally. This is idolatry: mistaking the means for the end. Fundamentalism is faith as archetypal possession. Our healthy and intelligent ego has become lost in the vast archetypal energy of the Self. It is a dangerous place because it splits life into good and evil, truth and falsehood, saved and unsaved. It allows no reconciliation of opposites, so necessary to spiritual maturity. It is unforgiving of those who see things differently from ourselves and can lead to hate and prejudice rather than love and inclusiveness. The Gaia movement, for instance, respects nature, but it goes astray when it sets up an opposition between the earth and us evil polluters. This is yet another attempt at splitting, imagining an all good energy and an all-evil energy. Life is not like that.

The reason nature can become God literally, as in pantheism, is because of its power to make us lose ourselves in something infinitely embracing and enduring. This loss of ego creates a more robust consciousness of oneness with all that is. That oneness in diversity feels like contact with the divine. In fact, the divine *is* just such seamless, egoless unity. The concept is authentic, but the conclusion is too literal. When "everything transitory is a metaphor," as Goethe says, the result is not pantheism but a subtle equation of irrefragable relatedness. This primordial and insuperable unity is the hypostatic union of the human with the divine.

As we become more adult about belief, we are more open to seeing things metaphorically. We no longer imagine that personifications are to be taken at face value. To say God is our father comes to mean God is like a father (and also like a mother) while still being beyond gender.

The life of Christ has historical foundation. But this is its most superficial level of appeal. Richer reality is in the analogy of Christ's life, death, and resurrection to our own personal journey. Every icon then becomes a mirror. We are continually seeing our own destiny acted out perfectly by Christ and the saints. This combination of historicity and metaphor is a quality of adult faith: "Their story is my story *and* their story has its own unique transcendent power and meaning." It is at once archetypal and truthful in itself.

What has always made faith specifically Christian is the belief in a historical fact behind the metaphor. It is no longer necessary to configure the word "history" so literally in the newsprint style of palpable fact. Jesus brings truth because what he did and what he said matches and enlivens the deepest archetypal truths of our being. In that sense, he *is* truth. That can be as legitimate a foundation of historical truth as any hard evidence. Truthfulness is the object of faith, not truth in a historically proven way.

Adult belief is articulated in the transformation of the ego and the loving action that follows it. The specific ingredient of difference for Christians is not the mythic message or the existential results. It is Jesus and his new life beyond death. But it does not have to be limited to him; it can include any and all the wonderful saints of human history. How the new life of Jesus happened or how it is still happening is a construction that changes from era to era as new philosophical models come and go. The other saints actually give us insight into how it happened and happens. Adult faith has a pantheon, not a single shrine.

Part of what helps us evolve as a species comes directly from faith. Centuries of faith have actually engendered a capacity in us to accomplish what we and our ancestors believe. Faith beliefs and rituals enshrine the evolved capacities of humanity that are not yet ready for recognition. Faith contains and preserves truths the psyche is not yet ready to know.

For instance, the Resurrection of Jesus signifies mastery over matter. Jesus' new life was not aimed at destroying or censuring matter but expanding it and enriching its role in the spiritual world. Gradually faith evolved from literal interpretations of this to metaphorical appreciation of it. As faith evolves, we do. Today we see a cooperation between spirit and matter. What began as a faith belief has now come true as a human potential that can be actualized. Faith holds our potential until we are ready to actualize it, and faith is one of the tools for that actualization. The key to it all is in the transition from literal interpretation to archetypal appreciation.

We notice greater compassion in the world today. We see more wisdom, more healing powers. The repeated acts of faith of our ancestors prepared us for this release of friendship with the universe. The new views in humanism came not only from science but also from faith. Religions come to be so that we might notice what is afoot in a realm that is more expansive than our ego. They present the divine milieu where unconditional love, perennial wisdom, and healing power are the ruling triumvirate. This is how the kingdom and the power and the glory belong to all of us.

3. Continual Revelations

As faith grows up there is no longer an attachment to a "deposit of faith" (a codex of dogmas requiring allegiance), but an appreciation of revelation as an ongoing happening. There is no final or exhaustive representation of truth. Revelation is not just an artifact of history. In the more dynamic articulation, revelation makes history and celebrates it every day. A person of faith reverences the scripture and the traditions of all human history as well as personal intuitive revelations that are happening interiorly here and now, especially those that can come from dreams and synchronicity.

As faith becomes more adult, it has less to do with a list of creedal declarations and more to do with trust. Jesus never asked anyone to recite a creed. Faith as described in the New Testament means confidence in Jesus and his message. The accent is on the establishment of a personal relationship, a trusting bond, not on a list of beliefs to which one gives assent. This is how devotion figures into the religious life. Relationship to Christ means that his life is our life, a life that demonstrates itself in compassionate love of everyone and in healing of the planet. To co-redeem is to revalue everything in his heart, to esteem everyone as worthy of generous love and attention.

"Christ lives in me" means I live his life here, now, that is, my ego is at the service of the Self with its commitment to unconditional love, perennial wisdom, and healing power. How I reckon theological statements is not relevant. Only living their truth is. St. Thomas Aquinas became a mystic after his vision of Jesus. He said that all his theological speculation was "like straw," compared to the experience of Christ in person. He appears in person every day when we engage in the works of mercy. (Seemingly unanswerable questions often have action answers in the works of mercy: "If there were a God, why does he permit children to starve?" My answer is: "I feed hungry children.")

4. A Conscience with Authority

As faith becomes more adult, we are no longer blindly obedient. We no longer swallow official Church pronouncements whole. Pronouncements based entirely on concepts from philosophy or tradition are much less relevant to adults than statements that reflect inner intuitive wisdom. The tradition of the Church is worthy of attention because it emerges from the ancestral memory of humankind. That same memory is in all of us.

As adults in faith we no longer center our life-choices on the apodictic injunctions of external authority. Instead, we are discerning about what is taught or proclaimed to us. We listen to a variety of theological opinions and draw the conclusions that make sense to us. Such discernment begins with the personal conviction that no religious authority has the right to tell us what we can or cannot read or see. We maintain and protect our right to full inquiry.

Our conscience has internal authority but is externally informed. The mature moral alternative to obedience is attention. Obedience is not a virtue in an adult. "I pay attention to what is taught but I always check in with myself and with persons I respect before I make a decision about something important. Official statements by the pope or bishops receive my attention in direct proportion to the extent to which they emerged from dialogue within the larger community and reflect what feels true in my own psyche."

With this approach, there are fewer problems with authority. As long as we remain angry at authority, we are in bondage to it and our anger turns to bitterness. To accept the need for authority in the human family is an adult accomplishment. To ask authorities to be responsible and to confront them when they overstep their boundaries is an adult challenge. The Church, after all, is not meant to parent us but to minister to us. It is not mother Church but friendly church and we are the friends.

To grow up in faith is to find and appreciate one's own voice, convictions, and worldview. These continually change and evolve throughout life. They may not always match the official Church teachings. Adults are willing to be heretics as long as they are flexible and open to altering their concepts and moral views. Free speech is a quality of adult religion, though it is not always easy to use, especially if one has an official status in the Church. Imaginative theologians may be silenced, and priests may be punished. An adult knows when to speak up, when to be silent by choice, and when to step out.

Finally, a healthy adult confronts the Church lovingly and sternly when its teachings cause pain, for example, on birth control and divorce, or when it excludes women, married men, and openly gay people from the priesthood. This does not mean banging one's head against the wall, but rather making one's statement, preferably in concert with others. An adult in faith will not wait a lifetime for change, only a few years. Do we stay in something that does not offer state-of-the-art religion and will not for the foreseeable future? Do we form our own small faith group? Each adult has to decide, and any sincere option is legitimate. We remain Catholics as long as we choose to be so in our hearts. No one can take that away from us.

5. Flexible but Informed

Adults look to recent scholarship and theology in order to enrich their faith. This means reading articles and books that present contemporary perspectives on belief and joining discussion groups. To limit one's intake of information to Sunday sermons, church bulletins, or diocesan newspapers does not broaden one's views. Adults are not satisfied with local or parochial opinions on any subject but rather go in search of a variety of ideas. They will not be satisfied with superficial knowledge but will look for more innovative ideas and more depth in the expression of them.

Adults put less credence in air-tight solutions to moral questions or "right answers" to doctrinal questions. They become satisfied with useful approximations. (What else do any of us have?) Jung says wisely: "Certitude does not lead to discovery." As faith becomes more adult there is less accent on absolutes. Instead there is a tolerance of ambiguity, a willingness to learn more, that is, "faith seeking understanding."

Adults are less definite and more flexible about formulating belief because they are not afraid of dismantling old ways of believing in favor of new constructions. These too may evolve and change with time. No belief has ever been stated perfectly for all time. *An adult does not possess a belief but follows it on its endlessly provocative path. Faith is more like a path than a platform.* Our maps are not the territory. Faith means certitude about realities, but how these realities will be expressed, understood, or conceptualized has enormous latitude. For centuries, Catholics were tied to a scholastic terminology that seemed itself part of faith. We are finally free of that and are opening ourselves to a variety of conceptual and experiential modes of approaching truth.

Adults want to let go of anything in their belief system that is still retrogressive and uninstructed. There is no contradiction between science and religion for an adult. Faith is a way of knowing what goes beyond and completes the deductive scientific method while still respecting it. The new physics acknowledges the wisdom of ancient spiritual traditions. Persons of faith educate themselves on how this integration of science and theology happens. As faith matures, for instance, we let go of the anachronistic worldview of an earth with heaven above and hell below. Such an antiquated cosmogony yields in adulthood to a perspective that is congruent with the scientific configuration of our own day and age.

An adult has beliefs that pass through phases, beliefs that reflect the dogmas of the Church but do not necessarily match them perfectly. An adult goes to a variety of sources and resources for faith understandings. *Catholics are those who are born and raised or converted to Catholicism and are now catholic in their sources and resources.*

6. Religious Politics

Clinging to sacraments or devotions with little or no social commitment is not faith. Christian faith is devotedness to Christ that acts itself out in living choices that show abiding love and loyal commitment to world concerns in nonviolent ways. True faith leads to progressively higher consciousness of the link between religious responsiveness and political exigencies. It does not begin or end in church. It begins in the heart and mind and ends in the real world. It is a letting go of the primacy of ego gratification in favor of the investment and subjection of our ego for the good of all.

As faith develops, we notice how much of what we have called belief is not conviction and commitment but sentiment and nostalgia. We may have a deep nostalgic bond (the bond of memory) to the Church and its traditions. This feels like heartfelt belief, but it may not be. It may be a romantic attachment based on the warm feelings associated with childhood consolations or family ties. It may be a way of validating our own identity, especially within our cultural context. "I am more truly Italian and thus more truly myself when I go to church." The bond is real faith when it is joined to existential commitment to Gospel principles that take me beyond my Italian biases and Italian ego.

7. Responsibility for Ourselves

We all have psychological work to do on ourselves. Religion is no substitute for it. Healthy religious life includes polishing our vessel, that is, clearing away old emotional unfinished business so that our psyche can be open more cleanly to faith. This psychological work takes effort. Assisting forces come our way in the form of good psychotherapists and any people who help facilitate our work. Grace appears in the form of automatic shifts to higher consciousness and as effortless spiritual serenity. This combination of steps we take and shifts we notice integrate our psychological and spiritual life so that faith can mature more readily.

To the maturing person, the mystery of God will be experienced as both fatherly and motherly. The sense of divine nurturance is not, however, a substitution of God for an unworthy, absent, or abusive parent. Adults work on their issues regarding parents in therapy through mourning and letting go. God as the "good father" in opposition to one's own "bad father" represents a denial of one's mortal experience and a loss of its potential for growth in character and depth. Jung says in *Psychology and Alchemy:* "The journey with father and mother up and down many ladders represents the making conscious of infantile contents that may have not yet been integrated. This personal unconscious must always be dealt with first — otherwise the gateway to the cosmic unconscious cannot be opened."

8. A New Worldview

As faith becomes more mature, we discern the difference between our own inherited cultural biases and authentic religious teaching. Love is letting go of biases against those whom we have been taught to hate or fear. Faith makes us see everything differently, feel more strongly, and give more generously. If we hold on to our inherited prejudices we are not really free enough for the work of faith.

Adult faith has made a radical difference in our way of seeing the world, our way of being in it, and our way of caring for it. Adult faith has made a radical difference in how we live, how we love, and how we think. It is entirely rooted in the Sermon on the Mount. If we still have the racial, gender, national, or sexual prejudices of our family or childhood, we do not have an adult faith since it has made no difference in our lives. Only when love makes a difference does religion have meaning. Here are the words of St. Aelred, a twelfth-century English abbot:

> You are good and lovable as you are. God is friendship and all the loves of your life are part of that great friendship for which you are eternally destined. . . . Create a small piece of paradise here on earth by loving and embracing each other and by loving and embracing the whole world. The cruelty, chaos, and pain of daily living cannot dim your vision of everlasting, perfect love as long as you cling to your precious friendships. (*The Earthly Paradise of Friendship*)

9. No More Magic

Part of our heritage may have been superstition (belief that omitting or committing certain actions automatically led to fortune or disaster). The nine first Fridays, the wearing of the scapular, became examples for Catholics of inherited superstitious beliefs and practices. Adults discredit any automatic link between a practice and a consequence though they may prayerfully intend or affirm a result. Magic and superstition mean that actions of ours can cause divine reactions. To believe that the wearing of a scapular means automatically that we will live to make a final confession is superstition. An adult recognizes that religious practices and objects prompt and manifest religious consciousness but do not cause it or insure a result from it.

"Magical thinking" is a characteristic of childhood. Adults discard magic from their mental and behavioral life. Magical thinking means equating our wishful beliefs or fears with reality: "I wish it, therefore it is true." Here are some of the characteristics of this kind of thinking. Ask yourself if any are familiar:

- Reality will match my picture of it.

- I am at the effect of forces that will erupt if I do not follow certain rules or rituals.

- If I arrange everything neatly or remain in control of everything I will be safe.

- There is only one way to or one source of happiness or safety.

- If an authority says it, it is true; otherwise it is not.

- If only this one thing would happen or be found or if only this one thing had not happened, everything would be perfect now.

- There is a scarcity of need-fulfilling objects. I must work hard and consider myself lucky to find the perfect one for me.

- Something has always been terribly wrong with me and it cannot be known, told, or fixed — though everyone else is aware of it.

- People will not love me or want me if they know me as I am.

- If I am guilty, I will be punished. If I am innocent, I will be exonerated.

- My behavior leads to unalterable consequences that no one can repair.

- I have done something too terrible to be forgiven.

- "What goes around, comes around." ("He'll get his" is a wish of the retaliatory ego, not a karmic certainty.)

- If I do not remain in control, everything will fall apart.

- I never win anything, or I will win if I take these ritual steps.

- If I talk about it openly, it will happen that way.

- It will not happen — or is not happening — if it is never mentioned.

- If a little is good, more is better.

- Happiness will not last if I enjoy it too much: "After laughter comes tears."

- Prosperity will be followed by catastrophe: "In a bull market, a bear is just around the corner."

At the same time we recall: "When Peter baptizes, Christ baptizes; when Judas baptizes, Christ baptizes." This saying points to the transcendent nature of sacramental power. It is not based on the person celebrating it but on the faith of the community. The old distinction between *ex opere operato* (from the act performed) and *ex opere operantis* (from the action of the one performing the act) refers to the value of a sacrament as an act of the Self not at the mercy of ego. It safeguards the power of a rite by separating it from the moral condition of the minister. This distinction is helpful because it shows the power of the believing community. But such a distinction would be magical if it were taken to mean that things work irrespective of human intention and attention. An adult has to let go of the childish view mentioned above, that human actions automatically cause divine results. That antiquated and magical view needs to be discarded in favor of the more mature perspective that gauges power by the depth of our focus *and* the grace present to us in the moment. Always, we are called to achieve and to receive.

10. No One Can Take It from Me

Once we grow up in faith, we can no longer be scandalized, that is, led to lose faith because of the malefactions of one of its representatives. The hierarchy and clergy will no longer be synonymous with the Church or perceived as the sole representatives of the Church. Their actions will be noticed and called to account if necessary. But their behavior or hypocrisy will not diminish our personal commitment to faith. Each person within each community will be thought of as representing the Church. Everyone will be viewed as having gifts and limits, being graced and sinful. The Church is all of us.

For an adult, the actions of a fellow believer or of an authority figure say absolutely nothing about the validity or meaning of the Church or its teachings. Those who have grieved over their religious past have no story left to tell about "that one priest who said or did that one thing that turned me off for good." No priest, minister, or nun can be invested with that power over adults who cherish their faith. In the same respect, adults do not base their faith on how kind or special a priest or minister was or is. Adult faith is grounded in an interior, personal, experiential contact with the Self, impervious to the actions of others. We truly have faith only when we believe that it has an enduring reality beyond people and their behavior, for good or ill.

11. Bodily Wisdom

"It is precisely in the spirit of celebration, gratitude, and joy that true purity is found," writes Thomas Merton. (What if *that* was what we heard in catechism class about purity?) As faith becomes more mature, we are less likely to see our own passions as dangerous and as requiring life-denying, suppressive control. Instead we celebrate our passions as powers of liveliness. We no longer fear our own bodies, instincts, impulses, or desires. We can handle them and enjoy them without violating our own or others' boundaries. The traditional restrictions of the Church on sexual behavior and insistence on constant self-denial were forms of abuse, an attempt to alienate us from our own bodies (the only vehicle we are given to live out our destiny). Adults take back their bodies and all bodily functions with care, responsibility, and joy. Our libido becomes recognizable as a spiritual power once it is free of ego fear and desire. *Which parts of your body are still in the hands of Rome?*

The patriarchal Eden story is about repression of sex, and shows no respect for mother earth. Hildegard of Bingen, a twelfth-century Benedictine abbess, proposed that Adam's sin was not allowing the activating of his erotic capacity to delight in the earth. We commit that sin when we condemn or fear sex. The faithwork is to find spiritual riches through our bodies, not in opposition to them.

It is important to distinguish sex and possession by sex. In the New Testament, the Greek word *soma* means "body." The word *sarx* means "flesh." "Flesh" has the specific connotation of possession by one's own lust and greed. It is only this that is condemned in the New Testament, never *soma*, body. The body is always spoken of with respect. To "hate the body" means to reject the authority of body over consciousness.

To let oneself become sexually addicted (obsessed with lust and irresponsibly, compulsively acting it out) is a from of idolatry. Sex becomes the All. (Attachment to vice of any kind erases our humanity. Greed, for instance, makes us heartless in our treatment or use of others.)

As faith becomes more adult, morality and belief are integrated. Mature morality pivots around values, not rules. This means that morality in sex is about accountability in sex, acting with adult consciousness, love, and respect for oneself and others. It does not make sex scary or evil, only challenging.

In the old self-abnegating approach, we were taught to distrust our sexual desires. The more holistic recommendation is to accept our sexuality and our sexual orientation as they are and then to design a

lifestyle that respects our inclination and yet is conscious and responsible. We thereby route our energies creatively and responsibly instead
of attempting to root them out. This means that morality is about
responsibility, not regulation.

As we grow in integrity we can trust an inner organismic (bodymind) wisdom that has a reliable moral sense. Thus sincere, morally
upright people today are choosing to live together before marriage.
Some believe that sex can occur with no intention to marry at all. Gay
Catholics are feeling free to act out their birthright of homoeroticism
and to establish long- or short-term homosexual bonds. People who see
themselves as inappropriately gendered choose operations that restore
them to a sense of harmony. Sex is no longer entirely about procreation
but about attention to one another in intimacy. Masturbation is now
viewed as appropriate in or out of relationship. What matters is adult
responsible behavior that reflects human needs and does not hurt oneself or others. Sexual behavior that takes advantage of youth, becomes
violent attack, or is manipulative is morally wrong.

The original values thus remain while individual lifestyles are pluralistic and have much more latitude in how they are expressed. This is not
a sign of a moral decline but of a moral upgrading. The Church contributed a sense of values to humanity, but when its rules become too
literal and fundamentalist, intelligent moral people design their own
choices in new ways. Our themes keep recurring: humans have religion
in them innately, part of which is moral behavior. People can cherish
the riches of theology while articulating them in ways that fit their own
current needs. This is how religious values are resources that transcend
repressive strictures and blind obedience.

12. Accountability

As faith becomes more adult, we experience appropriate guilt but
less and less neurotic guilt. True faith sets us free from shame and
self-blaming. Appropriate guilt is based on a break with one's own
conscientious integrity, which is admitted, amended, and let go of. Neurotic guilt may or may not be based on true reprehensibility, is or is not
admitted, is or is not amended, but is not let go of.

Appropriate guilt is based on accountability. Neurotic guilt is based
on fear. Neurotic guilt becomes an obsession with an underlying sense
of self-shame and serves no purpose. Appropriate guilt serves the purpose of clearing up something, redressing a wrong, rebalancing an
imbalance with full accountability. It is a process that ends with a sense

of having made progress personally and spiritually. Neurotic guilt is an interrupted process with no resolution or evolution. When faith is adult we no longer abuse ourselves with neurotic guilt but are free to live happily and responsibly. "Faith is the courage to accept our acceptability despite feelings of unacceptability," Paul Tillich says.

We free ourselves from guilt in a paradoxical way. We form a healthy and consistent conscience with a firm resolve to make amends when we fail. Then we have a way of processing guilt and transforming it. It is human and is not meant to vanish but to be a signal for correction. Frances Wickes writes, "If there is true self love, the judge becomes the redeemer, and the sense of judgment is lost in the miracle of transformation."

Morality means raiding the stores of love and dissolving the citadel of ego, the essence of psychological sanity and of spiritual sanctity. For an adult, there is less accent on rules and more on the rule of love. We act from joyful choice with great latitude and self-forgiveness. When faith is real it gives us flexibility and freedom. In fact, "the freedom of the sons of God" is the best indicator of a living faith. "Love and do what you will," St. Augustine says. Joseph Campbell adds: "The part of us that wants to become is fearless."

Abraham Maslow wrote: "The voice of the divine in us is counterpoised not by the voice of the devil but by the voice of fear." As faith matures, motivation for moral living changes from fearful obligation to loving choice. Fear is transformed into love. We no longer act or choose not to act because of the dread of the loss of heaven and the pains of hell. We act lovingly because we have come to realize that love is our very identity. Love has no motive; it is all we can do. When we love, we are being ourselves.

"God is love" then becomes experientially true and at the same time a metaphor for our True Self. We act in accord with the love within and around us; this is faithwork. Its infinite compassion makes us notice and feed the hungry as Jesus did. An identification has happened with Christ. "My I is God; I have no other me," says the mystic St. Catherine of Genoa. It is not that humanity is divinity or that one is the opposite of the other. There is a continuity of humanity and divinity as there is between mind and universe.

In adult faith, the trustful bond of faith is to a God of love and mercy, not to a God of judgment and punishment. St. Anselm's proposition was that God forgives only when he receives full satisfaction for sin. This archaic view can yield to one that certifies God's unconditional love, prompting forgiveness before restitution. In other words, those who are mature in faith feel unreservedly loved as they are, before, during, and after sin.

13. We Have Suffered Enough

When faith grows up, we no longer seek or absorb suffering. We no longer want to hurt ourselves or let ourselves be hurt. The old phrase "offer it up" is self-abnegating. It recommends powerlessness, nonassertiveness, passive absorption of pain. True spirituality is not possible with that kind of psychological dysfunctionality. The adult in faith approaches pain as an evil to be avoided, not as a goal to be sought or welcomed. The Alcoholics Anonymous prayer is an excellent example of the healthy adult view: "God, grant me the serenity to accept the things I cannot change, the courage to change the things I can, and the wisdom to know the difference." The only pain to be accepted and offered is that which has not responded to our attempts to relieve it. Always, health in spirituality builds on psychological health.

"Grace builds on nature," St. Thomas said. To be an adult means no longer seeing the "will of God" as an excuse for absorbing pain or for sitting back instead of standing up at attention. Edward Schillebeeckx says, "The will of God means blasphemy when it is the absolutizing of the status quo, of blind change, or of one's own view projected onto God." For an adult who has spiritual consciousness, "the will of God" simply means "what is" either after any attempts to change it have failed or after our efforts have succeeded in changing it. The final arrangement, the unalterable result, the redemption that happens beyond our human powers, the pain beyond our control: all represent dimensions of what is, and that can be called the will of God.

In the face of suffering, an adult seeks less the consolations of God and more the God of all consolation — who sometimes does not console. Adults do not "lose" their faith because of personal tragedy or desperation. In truly adult faith, dark events and periods are taken as givens of the volatility of life. An adult faith commitment is not based on "good feelings" but coexists with ever changing feelings or moods. Faith does not hinge on whether justice occurs in life or whether help comes one's way when needed. Considerations like that refer to the givens and vicissitudes of human life. Faith does not mean entitlement to a "special deal" or to immunity from the painful conditions of existence. To be adult in faith is to make a commitment to a message that challenges us to love with all our heart no matter what. To be an adult is to be grown up about loving, to let love reach its full stature in our every thought, word, and deed.

14. The Power of Prayer

As faith grows up, prayer changes. There is less accent on petitionary prayer, which often simply asks for support of the ego's view of what it needs. More accent in adult faith is on prayer as thanks for all that is and has been and yes to all that is and will be. In fact, thanks is a way of saying yes, a way of saying "Thy will be done." It is an assertion of the power of the Self over that of ego. To pray is to evoke the Self. This is what is meant by saying Christ prays in us; a larger life overrides our ego limits.

The covenant is an emblem of the conscious bond or axis between ego and Self. In this context, the ark is the psyche of humanity and of the universe. The concept of a chosen people in fact evokes the archetype of election, that is, with the support of the Self. Atheism means no invisible means of support. Prayer is a request for support. The humble ego seeks the guidance of the Self in prayer as the humble Self seeks the attention of the ego in the process of individuation. Prayer thus makes it possible for the ego in ordinary daily consciousness to touch the divine and be touched by it.

The attitude of thanksgiving and surrender means letting go of the grasping ego in favor of the emergence of the inner Self of wholeness, the true center of our identity that always reaches beyond itself with love. This makes prayer less a statement to Someone far from us. It is instead a staying in the spacious silence within our hearts where Jesus lives. To pray is to speak with his voice, to see with his eyes, to love with his heart. It is a continuous responsiveness to the Holy Spirit that groans with all the universe for the fulfillment of its destiny. To join that energy with ours is the prayer that grants a vision of existence that is no longer vectored by limits.

Affirmations are ways of expressing prayer. They declare what the psyche wants to have happen next on the spiritual path. Mindfulness meditation is a form of prayer because it releases us from ego and restores us to the present, the only point of departure for the soulful journey we humans are here to make. Thomas Merton discovered the value of Buddhist mindfulness practice in contemplation. The human potential movement and Eastern religions have added to the cornucopia of prayer techniques. They have provided valuable insights into the nature of prayer. It is not a way of changing or controlling or fixing things. It is a way of saying yes to what is. It is also a way of asking for what we need. It is not a demand with a "must have" energy. It is a serene abiding in what is with a willingness to let it be and a wish to let it change. In other words, prayer is the model of what it takes for wholeness in this fragmenting world.

> *My greatest weapon is silent prayer.*
> — Mahatma Gandhi

15. A Journey to Here

The spiritual journey is not from point A (our sinfulness) to point B (our redemption). It is all one emancipative journey of continually mended failures, reunion, and transformation. Our journey is from here to Here, from the here and now of our lives to the wider Here and Now of our destiny. This is how we create a condition "on earth as it is in heaven." Once there is room for all humankind in the heart of each of us, our work will not be to convince others of "the truth" but to bring the Church, that is, our best selves, to the world and to include the world in its embrace. Our struggle will not be to evangelize in the sense of proselytizing but to evangelize in the sense of the example we set by bringing love everywhere. Our work will be to feed the hungry, to clothe the naked, to shelter the shelterless, to visit the imprisoned. That will be the essence of evangelization. Such good news is really an awareness of precisely what makes the message of Jesus so different from any ever heard: salvation of ourselves happens through love of others. This is being saved from fear and finding love amid the ruins.

Conclusion: The Pilgrim's Progress

From time immemorial, men and women have gone on pilgrimages. Whether to Eleusis or Delphi, to Canterbury or Lourdes, human beings travel to shrines for healing of body and renewal of spirit. What is it about a shrine that is so appealing? How is a shrine a metaphor for our human journey? How does it reveal a recondite purpose?

Pilgrims travel to a shrine and from the shrine they travel home. Arrival at the shrine is thus the half-way point on the spiritual journey. It is the perfect pivotal center because it is both the goal that has been reached and the point of departure for another excursion, the one back to the quotidian home, this time with graces to share.

To arrive at the shrine took stamina and perseverance: so many hurdles on the way in the way. To leave the shrine takes courage. So many consolations, so abundantly afforded there. To remain kneeling at the shrine was our Western experience of devotion. To go from the shrine means returning to everyday reality but seeing it all newly radiant with light and bringing light to it. This is the Eastern view of "meditation in action." Thomas Merton helped us see how these two approaches complement and enrich each other. Every adult journey includes both. Faith cannot be complete at any single tradition or at any single shrine.

At first, a shrine can be misleading. We may think it honors an external God. Actually, it is a crossroads of divinity and humanity. It focuses our attention on a power that abides both beyond us and in us. Since all is one, those two come to the same reality in the last analysis, or rather in the present synthesis.

A shrine is a window and a mirror. Through it we glimpse God. In it we see a reflection of our own potential. Graces come to match and expand our unknown and unacknowledged capacities: "Your faith has made you whole." Miracles are both bestowed and evoked in this shrine to wholeness: the saint, the Bodhisattva, the fulfilled wholeness, has traveled the whole path and come back to help us along our path. Perhaps this tells us that it takes more than one lifetime to actualize our entire capacity to love, even longer to feel loved enough. Saints and Bodhisattvas come back repeatedly because it takes millennia to love us as much as we deserve or perhaps to have us become ready to receive the divine love that is always ours.

The candles radiate the light that defies darkness: a light to us and in us. The flowers honor the life that defies death: a life for us and in us. The larger-than-life size of the image and its celestial pose, the striking colors, incense, fabrics, wood, glass: all portray the divine in nature and in human art, one triune reality. All portray our human calling to be larger than we ever believed possible.

At the shrine, time stands still as do we. In that moment, travelers enter eternity in time to receive gifts to take back to time's world. Opposites unite at a shrine: time and the timeless, the human and the divine, the mortal and the immortal, the end and the beginning, even the light and the shadow. Yes, this much overwhelming goodness will always have beside it the presence of evil too, as Christ had Judas close by him at the Last Supper.

The wise traveler on the spiritual path is always aware that the brighter the light, the darker the shadow behind it. The saint warns the pilgrim of the dark side of the powers, as Christ, in raiment of snow, warned the disciples on high Tabor of the satanic darkness awaiting them below. Shrewd pilgrims, at the intersection of so many opposites, remain aware and on guard but confident and full of heart. They know there is a way to befriend the shadow and walk from the darkness into the light. The saint shows that and so does every hero story.

The shrine has shown the Path *and* the Paradise. It creates heaven on earth. It is the tableau of the invisible become at last and everlastingly visible. It is the goal and threshold of our work, promising a future that has already happened and that wants to happen again.

> *A true devoted pilgrim is not weary*
> *To measure kingdoms with his feeble steps.*
>
> — *The Two Gentlemen of Verona*

Epilogue

To let go of childhood beliefs does not have to mean the end of something. There are enduring archetypal values in our religious past that can be retained and reclaimed as our spiritual perspectives and practice mature. Our new-age spirituality seems to shy away from religion often in fear or distrust. This is a disservice to ourselves. There are precious riches in our childhood faith that wait to be recovered and then invested in our adult spirituality.

Integrating religion and spirituality is the threefold challenge explored in the preceding pages: we reconstruct the old familiar structures we inherited so they can be capacious enough to hold our lively, passionate, and evolving selves. We revision the perspectives of our present faith journey in the unlimited light of the contributions of all the religions, mythologies, psychology, and scholarship of our contemporary world and of history. We redraw the boundaries we were told not to cross so that we can expand our trust in our own consciences, free of repression.

If we do not stake our claim in just such courageous ways, we may lose what religion can give. More subtly and insidiously we may retain in our unconscious depths the inaccuracies, anachronisms, and fear or shame-based injunctions that others have left us. The task is to recover from the past and reclaim the riches of it. This takes the personal freedom to trespass, to grant ourselves the right to error in its literal sense of straying from the official path. These pages have attempted to show how all this can happen without venom or bitterness but with exuberance and effectiveness.

Childhood faith images remain in our psyche throughout our lives. This happens because they are associated with our personal and family memories but also because they reflect the deeper archetypal memories of the whole human family. Images hang on in us because they tune into truths always and already alive in our psyches. Such images carry meanings yet to be revealed or fathomed. Religious images and beliefs may also comfort us in the face of the harsh givens of human existence. Paying attention to all this helps us unravel it and befriend it. Reading this book was perhaps a form of such attentive befriending.

For those who have been away from the Church for a while, religion may sometimes seem like a broken cathedral after a bombing: here half a God, there half a Virgin. Beliefs can remain in us from childhood with no logical unity, based more on what had consoled us than on internal continuity or conscious choice. But it is never too late to find in the contradictory pieces something sufficient to begin a rebuilding. This is as legitimate as rebuilding a cathedral from its own ruins. We cannot live in these ruins, but we can begin again in them. The part of the cathedral that was made of wood has burned away. The part that was made of stone has remained. Our faith cathedral may look strange, as a single charred chimney looks strange after a fire has burned away a house. The challenge is to visit the ruins, to sit in the midst of them, to be fair witnesses of the devastation. Then, without pressure from the outside, we may decide to start reconstructing. A new Catholicism is stubbornly insisting on being born. We can be its midwives.

We may walk away for a while in grief or in anger and even try to dismiss the images of faith. This latter is the choice to be most wary of, since images remain in our conscious thoughts and imaginations because they still have something to tell, give, or ask us. Our destiny unfolds so much more smoothly when we honor the images that accompany and compose it. Jung says: "Whoever speaks in primordial images *evokes* the beneficent forces ... behind them."

Real faith comes to rest, as St. Thomas Aquinas suggests, not in adherence to beliefs or in devotional feelings but in generous and compassionate action. True faith in the Gospel of Jesus is summarized by him in Matthew 25:31–46. Here he says that the kingdom is for those who feed the hungry, shelter the shelterless, clothe the naked, and visit the sick and imprisoned. Faith is shown first of all in having and showing love for everyone. The work of adult faith is unconditional and universal love. In this way, faith is a driving force of our evolution as beings of integrity and compassion. Every one of us on a spiritual path has faith. We believe in the reality of something we cannot prove or see.

Ruins offer the promise of renewal since opposites continually constellate in the psychic world and life is ever renewing itself in the natural world. These worlds are one. To rebuild from the ruins of our religious past is to find support for our evolving spirituality and for this commitment to love in our familiar religious images, beliefs, and rituals. This can happen while in a church community or outside one. Rejoining the Church makes sense if it supports personal and spiritual development. A twelve-step program comes to mind as an example of such a community.

Catholicism does not stop us now, but it can be how we stop ourselves. This book has been about what it offers that can contribute to a mature spiritual consciousness. Our spirituality does not mature simultaneously with our other areas of development. We do not grow up in any area unless we are fed. Our intellect does not grow automatically in knowledge. It requires attention and the food of information, intuition, and experience. Faith does not grow up unless it is nourished. It sometimes takes many years to know which foods are best for our body, and it can take many years to know which spiritual foods nurture our spirituality. It takes a journey, sometimes outside our origins, to find out what is best for us.

The best behavior of a human ego is the virtues. The ego has a dark side: self-centered, arrogant, vindictive, controlling. The sports of this unhealthy ego are the vices, the seven deadly sins. Religion works for us in this arena. It offers human-enhancing beliefs, intelligent morality (restraint, virtue, altruism, and amends when necessary), cogent rituals of initiation and transition, and personal devotion. These are four of the fundamental religious instincts in us that fulfill the inner needs of each phase of life. "Losing our faith" may simply mean that we no longer see membership in an institutional church as necessary but the four elements of the religious instinct still press their claims upon us.

The criminal risking we see in young people today is a poignant indicator of their thirst for initiation. The world needs youthful energy as much as it needs the wisdom of age. Youth becomes frustrated and destructive when we offer no way to channel its energy in meaningful ways. The sacraments as we read them from the *Ritual* can be redesigned to fit contemporary realizations and needs. Then they will be restored as initiation rites.

The year 2000 is a jubilee year for the Catholic Church. Its true jubilee will happen not in the fanfare of Rome but when the Church finally becomes catholic. The pages that are ending now have shown some ways that can happen. The central way is to restore three glittering jewels to the crown of Catholicism. The first is the recognition that religion begins as an intrapsychic event, the contribution of Jung. The second is that nature is the locus of divine life, the contribution of contemporary science. The third is the teaching and meditation practice of Buddhism, pioneered in Christianity by Thomas Merton. All three of these have always been part of Roman Catholic tradition, thanks to the mystics.

Our Catholic past was tied to the classical Greek philosophical tradition. It emphasized the omnipotence of logic and reason over intuition and vision. It left little or no room for feeling and intuition in the search for truth. It gave priority to logic as sufficient for certainty. It reduced mystery to that which reason could not account for or explain. At the same time, contradictorily, it denied the legitimacy of personal search in favor of authority. In the Middle Ages, authority and systematic theology had gained full hegemony. Our heritage of religion was almost entirely synonymous with Greek philosophy via Plato and Aristotle, thus diminishing its room for the mystical, the intuitive, the miraculous, the archetypal: all the avenues that connect us to the transcendent and reveal the unity that saints extol.

A truly mature religious attitude is transphilosophical and trans-institutional. That is the meaning of "that all may be one." It is not that all traditions have to fold into Catholicism but that anyone can become truly catholic, that is, universal, in our respect for truth. This reflects the style of evolution. It is not directed toward unity but toward synthesis. The criterion for a healthy religious attitude is one that unites all traditions without having to abandon one to join another. Traditions are not adversarial but complementary. (The Church is the great matchmaker since it joined us to so many other traditions by reason of its own narrowness. The Church of our childhood forced us to look elsewhere, everywhere.)

Religion today cannot be limited to the scripture and tradition of one Church. It has to include the best of depth and archetypal psychology, oriental wisdom, the new spiritually conscious physics, humanism, the newest biblical and historical scholarship, and insights and practices from any of the religions of humankind. Thich Nhat Hanh says: "When you are a truly happy Christian, you are a Buddhist also. And vice versa.... On the altar of my hermitage are images of Buddha and Jesus, and I touch both of them as my spiritual ancestors." The silence of the Holy Spirit in the soul is the same as the silence of Buddha under the bo tree.

Formerly, we were limited to Catholic sources, but now we can open ourselves to the wide world of wisdom that cuts across time and religious persuasions. Intelligent people insist on that total access. This is using the whole compass on the spiritual path, and every direction points to nurturance, not just one. Empowerment means finally grasping that everything is spacious, that there is room in us for more than our own past, our own belief system, our own loyalties. We can be Catholics who follow a Buddhist path of meditation, respect the social consciousness of humanism, and simultaneously rejoice in the newest advances of physics. To draw from more than one tradition does not have to confuse or split us. The identity of an apricot tree is not split by being grafted to another so that a higher quality of fruit can result.

John Dunne, a Catholic theologian, says: "When one is no longer concerned about reaching agreement and restoring confidence in one's own culture, life, and religion, but simply about attaining insight and understanding, then one can enter freely into other cultures, lives, and religions and come back to understand one's own in a new light."

In today's world, the complex relationship between human and divine can no longer be mediated by any single voice or tradition. Awareness of the great varieties of the spiritual life has grown too great to permit such limitation. Since the truth is within, the *personal* religious experience of every one of us is as valid as that of St. John of the Cross. Something happened to him as himself and to me as myself. To be catholic is to trust that freedom and right. All living things keep changing. Only dead things remain unaltered.

Once the Church is ourselves, we work together as a confraternity with a common experience and a common mission: to respect our religious past for its treasures and to design a religious future with them as a foundation but not the only one. "Those who are at the heart of their different religions are closer to one another than they are to those who are at the fringes," wrote C. S. Lewis.

Max Planck remarked that old beliefs die when old believers die. We cannot wait for the institutional Church to catch up to catholicity. It is the nature of an institution to lag behind the times. Our task is to salvage and preserve what it has of value and truth. Our work is to let reality break through its traditional vehicles: the Bible, the sacraments, the creed. The challenge is to let old pledges pay off in modern tender.

This book proposes a liberated Catholicism. It is tempting to call oneself a liberal Catholic as distinguished from a fundamentalist Catholic. But the working principle has to be pluralism, not division. This book has not been for or against religion but about its values, assets, and limitations. We distinguish the religious instinct of reverence from the fear of hell, religious images mirroring the depths of our souls from antiquated ones that have lost their living relevance, religious rituals enacting initiation from institutionalism, repression, and empty forms. *Can I accept the ecological challenge to use the fossil fuels of* my religious dinosaurs to ride into the new millennium? This century divided religion from spirituality. Can the next reconnect them sanely and lovingly?

You never enjoy the world aright, till the sea itself flows in your veins, till you are clothed with the heavens, and crowned with the stars: and perceive yourself to be the sole heir of the whole world, and all are sole heirs with you. Your enjoyment of the world is never right, till every morning you awake in heaven: see yourself in your Father's palace, and look upon the skies, the earth and the air as celestial joys: having such a reverend esteem of all as if you were among the angels.

You never enjoy the world aright, till your spirit fills the whole world, and the stars are your jewels, . . . till you are intimately acquainted with that shady night out of which the world was made, till you love others so as to desire their happiness, with a thirst equal to the zeal for your own . . . and rejoice in the palace of your glory, as if it had been made today this morning. You never enjoy the world aright till you so love the beauty of enjoying it that you are earnest to have others enjoy it too. You never enjoy the world aright, till you see all things in it so perfectly yours, that you cannot desire them any other way: and till you are convinced that all things serve you best just as they are.

Love is the true means by which the world is enjoyed: our love for others and their love for us. . . . If we cannot be satisfied by love, we cannot be satisfied at all. Never was any thing in this world loved too much . . . but only in too short a measure.

At my birth, I was a little stranger, saluted and surrounded with innumerable joys. All things were glorious, yea, and infinitely mine. . . . Everything was at rest, free, and immortal. All time was eternity. There was an immortal wheat, which never should be reaped, nor was ever sown. I thought it must have stood from everlasting to everlasting.

The dust and stones of the street were as precious as gold, the gates were the beginning and the end of the world. The green trees . . . made my heart to leap and go almost mad with ecstasy; they were such strange and wonderful things. The city seemed to stand in Eden. The streets were mine; the temple was mine; the people were mine; the skies were mine and so were the sun and the moon and stars. The delights of Paradise were round about me. Heaven and earth were open to me.

Like the sun we dart our rays before us, and occupy those spaces with light and contemplation which we move towards but possess not.

The All is wholly within us and even then seems wholly without us. The place wherein the world stands, were it all annihilated, would still remain, the endless extent of which we feel so really and so palpably, that we do not more certainly know the distinctions and bounds of what we see, than the everlasting expansion of what we feel and behold within us. It is an object infinitely great and ravishing: as full of treasures as full of room, as full of joy as of capacity. To blind men it may seem dark, but it is all glorious within, infinite in light. Everyone is alone the center and circumference of it.

— THOMAS TRAHERNE,
seventeenth-century Anglican mystic,
from his book *Centuries of Meditation*

Bibliography

Works Consulted

Abbott, Walter, ed. *The Documents of Vatican II.* New York: America Press, 1966.

Baum, Gregory. *Man Becoming: God in Secular Experience.* New York: Herder and Herder, 1971.

———. *Religion and Alienation: A Theological Reading of Sociology.* New York: Paulist Press, 1975.

———. *Sociology and Human Destiny: Essays on Sociology, Religion and Society.* New York: Crossroad, 1980.

Bellah, Robert. *Beyond Belief.* New York: Harper and Row, 1970.

Bellah, Robert, et al. *The Good Society.* New York: Knopf, 1991.

Berger, Peter L. *A Rumor of Angels: Modern Society and the Rediscovery of the Supernatural.* New York: Doubleday, 1969.

Berry, Thomas. *The Dream of the Earth.* San Francisco: Sierra Club Books, 1988.

Bohm, David, and David Peat. *Science, Order, and Creativity.* New York: Bantam, 1987.

Booth, Leo. *When God Becomes a Drug: Breaking the Chains of Religious Addiction and Abuse.* Los Angeles: Tarcher, 1991.

Borchert, Bruno. *Mysticism: Its History and Challenge.* York Beach, Maine: Weiser, 1994.

Boswell, John. *Christianity, Social Tolerance, and Homosexuality.* Chicago: University of Chicago Press, 1980.

Brown, Peter. *The Body and Society: Men, Women and Sexual Renunciation in Early Christianity.* New York: Columbia University Press, 1988.

Bruteau, Beatrice. *God's Ecstasy: The Creation of a Self-Creating World.* New York: Crossroad, 1997.

Campbell, Joseph. *Hero with a Thousand Faces.* Princeton: Princeton University Press, 1968.

———. *The Masks of God: Creative Mythology.* New York: Penguin, 1968.

———. *Transformations of Myth through Time.* New York: Harper and Row, 1990.

Capra, Fritjof. *The Tao of Physics.* Boston: Shambhala, 1975.

———. *Uncommon Wisdom.* New York: Simon and Schuster, 1988.

Carr, Ann. *Transforming Grace: Christian Tradition and Women's Experience.* San Francisco: Harper and Row, 1988.

Chagdud, Tulku. *Gates to Buddhist Practice*. Junction City, Calif.: Padma, 1993.

Cooke, Bernard. *Sacraments and Sacramentality*. Mystic, Conn.: Twenty-Third Publications, 1983.

Corbett, Lionel. *The Religious Function of the Psyche*. London: Routledge, 1996.

Corless, Roger. *I Am Food: The Mass in Planetary Perspective*. New York: Crossroad, 1981.

Cornell, Judith. *Mandala*. Wheaton, Ill.: Quest, 1994.

Crosby, Michael H. *Dysfunctional Church: Addiction and Co-Dependency in the Family of Catholicism*. Notre Dame, Ind.: Ave Maria Press, 1991.

Curran, Charles E. *Directions in Catholic Social Ethics*. Notre Dame, Ind.: University of Notre Dame Press, 1985.

De Mello, Anthony. *Awareness: A De Mello Spirituality Conference in His Own Words*. New York: Doubleday, 1990.

Dolan, Jay. *The American Catholic Experience: A History from Colonial Times to the Present*. New York: Doubleday, 1985.

Donnelly, Doris. *Mary, Woman of Nazareth*. Mahwah, N.J.: Paulist Press, 1989.

Dossey, Larry. *Healing Words: The Power of Prayer and the Practice of Medicine*. San Francisco: Harper, 1993.

Dourley, John P. *The Illness That We Are: A Jungian Critique of Christianity*. Toronto: Inner City Books, 1984.

———. *A Strategy for a Loss of Faith: Jung's Proposal*. Toronto: Inner City Books, 1992.

Dulles, Avery. *Models of the Church*. New York: Doubleday, 1987.

Edinger, Edward. *The Christian Archetype: A Jungian Commentary on the Life of Christ*. Toronto: Inner City Books, 1987.

———. *Ego and Archetype*. Boston: Shambhala, 1992.

Eliade, Mircea. *Rites and Symbols of Initiation: The Mysteries of Birth and Rebirth*. New York: Harper, 1958.

———. *The Sacred and the Profane: The Nature of Religion*. New York: Harcourt, Brace, 1959.

———. *Myth and Reality*. New York: Harper and Row, 1963.

———. *The Myth of the Eternal Return*. Princeton: Princeton University Press, 1965.

Feinstein, David, and Stanley Krippner. *Personal Mythology: The Psychology of Your Evolving Self*. Los Angeles: Tarcher, 1988.

Fox Matthew, O.P. *Original Blessing*. Santa Fe: Bear & Co., 1983.

———. *Sins of the Spirit, Blessing of the Flesh*. New York: Harmony, 1999.

Glazer, S., ed. *The Heart of Learning: Spirituality and Education*. New York: Tarcher, 1999.

Greeley, Andrew. *The Catholic Experiment*. New York: Doubleday, 1967.

Hanh, Thich Nhat. *Living Buddha, Living Christ*. New York: Putnam-Riverhead Books, 1995.

Hannah, Barbara. *Encounter with the Soul: Active Imagination*. Boston: Sigo Press, 1981.

Hellwig, Monika. *Christian Women in a Troubled World*. New York: Paulist Press, 1985.

Hennessey, James. *American Catholics: A History of the American Catholic Church in the United States*. New York: Oxford, 1981.

Houston, Jean. *Godseed: The Journey of Christ*. Wheaton, Ill.: Quest, 1992.

Hubbard, Barbara Marx. *Conscious Evolution: Awakening the Power of Our Social Potential*. Novato, Calif.: New World Library, 1998.

James, William. *The Varieties of Religious Experience*. New York: Simon & Schuster, 1997.

Jung, Carl, et al. *Man and His Symbols*. New York: Doubleday, 1964.

———. *Psychology and Religion: West and East*. New York: Princeton University Press, 1969.

Keating, Thomas. *The Mystery of Christ: The Liturgy as a Religious Experience*. Rockport, Mass.: Element, 1987.

———. *Awakenings*. New York: Crossroad, 1990.

———. *Crisis of Faith, Crisis of Love*. Vol. 1. New York: Continuum, 1995.

———. *Active Meditations for Contemplative Prayer*. New York: Continuum, 1997.

Kemp, C., and D. Pologrutto. *Catholics Coming Home: A Handbook for Churches Reaching Out to Inactive Catholics*. San Francisco: Harper, 1990.

Küng, Hans. *Christianity: Essence, History, and Future*. New York: Continuum, 1995.

Lama, Dalai. *Kindness, Clarity, and Insight*. Ithaca. Snow Lion, 1988.

———. *Opening the Eye of New Awareness*. Boston: Wisdom, 1999.

Lovelock, J. E. *Gaia: A New Look at Life on Earth*. Oxford: Oxford University Press, 1979.

McBrien, Richard. *Catholicism*. Minneapolis: Winston, 1980.

McCool, Gerald, ed. *Rahner Reader*. New York: Crossroad, 1975.

Merton, Thomas. *Conjectures of a Guilty Bystander*. New York: Doubleday, 1968.

———. *Zen and the Birds of Appetite*. New York: New Directions, 1968.

Miller, Alice. *The Drama of the Gifted Child*. New York: Basic Books, 1981.

Moore, R. L., ed. *Carl Jung and Christian Spirituality*. Mahwah, N.J.: Paulist, 1988.

Moore, R. L., and D. J. Meckel, eds. *Jung and Christianity in Dialogue*. Mahwah, N.J.: Paulist, 1990.

Moore, Sebastian. *The Fire and the Rose Are One*. New York: Seabury, 1980.

Moreno, A. *Jung, Gods, and Modern Man*. Notre Dame, Ind.: University of Notre Dame Press, 1970.

Murray, Peter. *Art of the Renaissance*. New York: Thames and Hudson, 1985.

Nolan, Albert. *Jesus before Christianity*. Rev. ed. Maryknoll, N.Y.: Orbis, 1992.

Occhiogrosso, Peter. *Once a Catholic*. Boston: Houghton Mifflin, 1987.

O'Neal, David. *Meister Eckhart: From Whom God Hid Nothing*. Boston: Shambhala, 1996.

Otto, Rudolf. *The Idea of the Holy*. Oxford: Oxford University Press, 1950.

Powers, Joseph. *Spirit and Sacrament: The Humanizing Experience*. New York: Seabury, 1973.

Ranke-Heinemann, U. *Eunuchs for the Kingdom of Heaven: Women, Sexuality, and the Catholic Church*. New York: Penguin, 1990.

Richo, David. *Unexpected Miracles: The Gift of Synchronicity and How to Open It.* New York: Crossroad, 1998.

———. *Shadow Dance: Liberating the Power and Creativity of Your Dark Side.* Boston: Shambhala, 1999.

Rollins, Wayne. *Jung and the Bible.* Atlanta: John Knox Press, 1983.

Schachter-Shalomi, R. Z. *Paradigm Shift.* Northvale, N.J.: Jason Aronson, 1993.

Schillebeeckx, Edward. *Church: The Human Story of God.* New York: Crossroad, 1991.

Sheldrake, Rupert. *The Rebirth of Nature.* New York: Bantam, 1991.

Smith, Huston. *The World's Religions.* San Francisco: Harper, 1991.

Steindl-Rast, David. *Gratefulness, the Heart of Prayer: An Approach to Life in Fullness.* Mahwah, N.J.: Paulist, 1984.

Steindl-Rast, David, Capra Fritjof, and Thomas Matus. *Belonging to the Universe: Explorations of the Frontiers of Science and Spirituality.* San Francisco: Harper, 1991.

Tarnas, Richard. *The Passion of the Western Mind: Understanding the Ideas That Have Shaped Our Western View.* New York: Harmony, 1991.

Teilhard de Chardin, Pierre. *The Phenomenon of Man.* New York: Harper & Row, 1975.

———. *The Divine Milieu.* New York: Harper & Row, 1982.

Thurman, Robert. *Essential Tibetan Buddhism.* San Francisco: Harper, 1995.

Trungpa, Chogyam. *Cutting through Spiritual Materialism.* Boston: Shambhala, 1987.

Warner, Marina. *Alone of All Her Sex: The Myth and the Cult of the Virgin Mary.* New York: Knopf, 1976.

White, Victor. *God and the Unconscious.* Dallas: Spring Publications, 1982.

Wickes, Frances. *The Inner World of Choice.* New York: Harper, 1963.

Wilber, Ken. *Eye to Eye: The Quest for the New Paradigm.* New York: Harper, 1983.

———. *The Marriage of Sense and Soul: Integrating Science and Religion.* New York: Random House, 1998.

DAVID RICHO, PH.D., is a psychotherapist and teacher in Santa Barbara and in San Francisco, California. He is the author of:

How to Be an Adult

When Love Meets Fear

Unexpected Miracles: The Gift of Synchronicity and How to Open It

Shadow Dance: Liberating the Power and Creativity of Your Dark Side

Dr. Richo gives workshops across the country, and some of these are audiotaped. For a catalog of his tapes and books send a self-addressed, single-stamped, legal-sized envelope to:

DR
Box 31027
Santa Barbara, CA 93130

The catalog may also be accessed on the web at
http://members.aol.com/davericho